More Praise for
NEIGHBOR

"Compact, sharp and withering. . . . Like an oral tale transcribed by a folklorist, it has the ring of the eternal to it. My tale is simple and horrible, it seems to say; listen to it and remember it and pass it along. Hatred like this runs deep in human nature and is ever ready to erupt again. Be warned."

—MICHAEL FRANK, *Los Angeles Times*

"Powerful. . . . Extraordinary."

—JAROSLAV ANDERS, *New Republic*

"Horrifying and thoughtful."

—ISTVÁN DEÁK, *New York Review of Books*

"*Neighbors* strikes squarely at Poland's accepted historical narrative."

—JOHN REED, *Financial Times*

"[A] scrupulously documented study."

—ABRAHAM BRUMBERG, *Times Literary Supplement*

"*Neighbors* tells a compelling story admirably. It should be widely read and discussed, for the complex, unsettling issues it raises still need to be fully explored."

—ALVIN H. ROSENFELD, *New Leader*

"[Gross] is possessed of the key . . . virtues: moral energy, commitment to accuracy, and the maintenance of a continuing open dialogue between historian, sources and reader."

—INGA CLENDINNEN, *London Review of Books*

"Compelling. . . . Gross's dispassionate book is the most comprehensive effort to uncover the stark truth about Jedwabne."

—ROBERT S. WISTRICH, *Commentary*

"*Neighbors* is a truly pathbreaking book, the work of a master historian. Jan Gross has a shattering tale to tell, and he tells it with consummate skill and control. The impact of his account of the massacre of the Jews of Jedwabne by their Polish neighbors is all the greater for the calm, understated narration and Gross's careful reconstruction of the terrifying circumstances in which the killing was undertaken. But this little book is much, much more than just another horror story from the Holocaust. In his imaginative reflections upon the tragedy of Jedwabne, Gross has subtly recast the history of wartime Poland and proposed an original interpretation of the origins of the postwar Communist regime. This book has already had dramatic repercussions in Poland, where it has single-handedly prised open a closed and painful chapter in that nation's recent past. But *Neighbors* is not only about Poland. It is a moving and provocative rumination upon the most important ethical issue of our age. No one who has studied or lived through the twentieth century can afford to ignore it."
—TONY JUDT, author of *Postwar: A History of Europe since 1945*

"This tiny book reveals a shocking story buried for sixty years, and it has set off a round of soul searching in Poland. But the questions it raises are of universal significance: How do 'ordinary men' turn suddenly into 'willing executioners?' What, if anything, can be learned from history about 'national character?' Where do we draw the line between legitimately assigning present responsibility for wrongs perpetrated by previous generations and unfairly visiting the sins of the fathers on the children? The author has no facile answers to these problems, but his story asks us to think about them in new ways."
—DAVID ENGEL, author of *The Holocaust: The Third Reich and the Jews*

"This is unquestionably one of the most important books I have read in the last decade both on the general question of the mass murder of the Jews during World War II and on the more specific problem of the reaction of Polish society to that genocide. All of the issues it raises are handled with consummate mastery. I finished this short book both appalled at the events it describes and filled with admiration for the wise and all-encompassing skill with which the painful, difficult, and complex subject has been handled."
—ANTONY POLONSKY, Brandeis University

NEIGHBORS

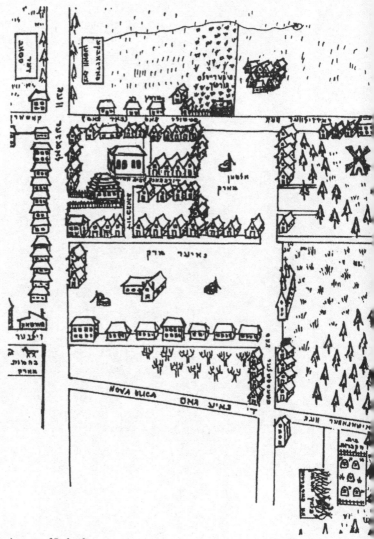

A map of Jedwabne
drawn by Julius Baker
(Yehuda Piekarz).

JAN T. GROSS

With a new preface by the author

The

Destruction

of the Jewish

Community

in Jedwabne,

Poland

NEIGHBORS

PRINCETON UNIVERSITY PRESS   PRINCETON AND OXFORD

First published by Princeton University Press in 2001
First paperback edition by Penguin in 2002
New paperback edition, with a new preface by the author, by
Princeton University Press, 2022

Paper ISBN 9780691234304
ISBN (ebook) 9780691234311

Library of Congress Control Number: 2021948924

This book has been composed in Janson

Cover design by Lauren Michelle Smith

press.princeton.edu

Printed in the United States of America

Fellow citizens, we cannot escape history.

—Abraham Lincoln,
  Annual Message to Congress
  DECEMBER 1, 1862

CONTENTS

Preface to the 2022 Edition   ix

Acknowledgments   xxxvii

Introduction   3

Outline of the Story   14

Sources   23

Before the War   33

Soviet Occupation, 1939–1941   41

The Outbreak of the Russo-German War
and the Pogrom in Radziłów   54

Preparations   72

Who Murdered the Jews of Jedwabne?   79

The Murder   90

Plunder   105

Intimate Biographies   111

Anachronism   122

What Do People Remember?   126

Collective Responsibility   132

New Approach to Sources   138

Is It Possible to Be Simultaneously a Victim and a Victimizer?   143

Collaboration   152

Social Support for Stalinism   164

For a New Historiography   168

Postscript   171

Notes   205

Index   249

PREFACE TO THE 2022 EDITION

This paperback edition of *Neighbors*, to my delight, is being published twenty years after the book came out at Princeton University Press. The book's trajectory so far—*habent sua fata libelli*—has been rather remarkable. Translated into thirteen languages, it was read widely and debated extensively, nowhere more so than in Poland. Alongside criticism, accompanied at times with acerbic personal attacks against the author, *Neighbors* also received its share of acclaim. The recognition I liked best was when Princeton University Press celebrated its own centenary and listed *Neighbors* among the one hundred books it treasured most. A small poster issued on the occasion included my photograph from the back cover together with many clever and sympathetic faces, such as a likeness of Albert Einstein.

I had been publishing books about the experience of the Second World War in Poland, under both the German and the Soviet occupation, for twenty-five years before I wrote *Neighbors.*[1] Of course, I could not have written it until I came across the requisite documentation. But the reasons for the delay were also deeper, rooted in the manner historians were writing about the war and the Shoah.

It may seem hardly conceivable nowadays, when books about various aspects of the Holocaust are published in abundance, that the mass murder of European Jews was in postwar decades a subject shunned by scholars. The reasons for it were multiple, having to do not only with the difficulty of contemplating the enormity of crimes committed, but also, I suspect, with the reluctance to confront different shades of complicity in Nazi-engineered evil by peoples and institutions in German-occupied Europe. With elegant restraint, in his magisterial study, Saul Friedländer put it thus: "Not one social group, not one religious community, not one scholarly institution or professional association in Germany and throughout Europe declared its solidarity with the Jews . . . ; to the contrary, many . . . were directly involved in the expropriation of the Jews and eager, be it out of greed, for their wholesale disappearance. Thus *Nazi and related anti-Jewish policies could unfold to their most extreme levels without the interference of any major countervailing interests*."[2] "[F]or much of the war," another historian had written, "Europeans fell into line and contributed what [the Germans] demanded anyway. After 1945, this was conveniently forgotten."[3]

This, I presume, must have had initially a chilling effect on academic engagement with the Shoah, and it took a long time before extermination of the Jews emerged as a widely pursued subject of scholarly research. When Raul Hilberg decided to write his doctoral dissertation at Columbia University in New York in the early 1950s—it would become the founding classic in Holocaust studies, *The Destruction of the European Jews*—his academic adviser, Franz Neumann (like Hilberg, an exiled Austrian Jew and an early student of Nazi totalitarianism), warned him that with such a topic for a PhD thesis he stood little chance of getting a university appointment. Against considerable skepticism of fellow academics—Hannah Arendt, for instance, in a rare lapse of judgment, advised Princeton University Press to turn it down—Hilberg's book finally came out in 1961 at a small publisher, Quadrangle Books, thanks to a subsidy from a private benefactor.

It was not the unavailability of data that made the scholarly community reluctant to engage with the subject. Jewish inhabitants of East European ghettos had launched several initiatives to document the process of extermination while the killings were still going on. The best known was the so-called Oneg Shabbat archive in the Warsaw ghetto—a systematic team effort to compile documents, interview witnesses, and carry out surveys under the leadership of the historian and social activist Emanuel Ringelblum.[4] And then, in the immediate aftermath of the war, beginning in the earliest moments after the remnants of European Jewry emerged from hideouts and concentration camps, again a documentation effort was launched as Holocaust survivors were prompted by a nucleus of Jewish historians, social workers, and activists to write down, collect, and record their testimonies.

Whether in Poland or in the displaced persons refugee camps (primarily in the American zone of occupation in Germany, where tens of thousands of Jewish survivors fled from the postwar upsurge of anti-Semitism in their own countries),[5] Jewish organizations, while dispensing aid, were compiling documentation of the genocide that had just wiped out the lives of six million European Jews. In Poland alone, where the destruction of Jewish organized life was particularly thorough, the Central Jewish Historical Commission, active since the end of 1944 under the auspices of the umbrella welfare organization called the Central Committee of Jews in Poland, assembled over seven thousand testimonies. Today they are housed in the archives of the Jewish Historical Institute in Warsaw, where I read Szmul Wasersztajn's statement, the starting point for reconstructing the mass murder in Jedwabne.

And there were more efforts to assemble and publish evidence about the Shoah immediately after the war. Scores of Jewish journalists who had emigrated from Eastern Europe before the war rushed back as soon as

Hitler had been defeated in order to find out and report what had happened. They had an eager and desperate audience—the readers of Yiddish language press on all the continents—who pined for any scrap of information about their communities of origin and the fate of relatives. A flood of brilliant reporting about the Shoah followed, with New York's daily *Forverts* being the leading venue for such writing. A recent Polish-language edition of a collection of Mordechai Tsanin's postwar articles in that newspaper shows what a comprehensive body of knowledge about the Holocaust was available in the public domain at the time.[6] As a result of all these efforts, continuing until the present day, the Holocaust is undoubtedly the best-documented genocide ever.[7]

And yet—despite all the available evidence—decades passed before historians took on the subject. Among the reasons was also a deep skepticism, indeed the rejection, on methodological grounds, of personal testimonies as a reliable source for historical research. Hilberg was an early advocate of this position: people's recollections are subjective, and hence open to criticism as unreliable, and they are not even needed to show the immensity of the Nazi criminal project, which can be demonstrated on the basis of "objective," institutionally generated documentation. He proceeded in this fashion, wrote a foundational book in the field, and a paradigm was set.

Once academic research on the destruction of European Jewry was set in motion (the terms "Holocaust" and "Shoah" would emerge much later), the subject was framed as a confrontation between Jews and Germans. This, of course, captured the gist of Nazi German genocidal policies launched against the Jews in occupied Europe. But in time such a conceptualization began to show its limitations. To be sure, the German-organized mechanisms and apparatus of destruction was the kernel of the mass-killing process, but it was also becoming clear to scholars that the local context mattered. Jews lived for centuries enmeshed in European societies, and they had to be extricated therefrom in order to be put or sent to death. Clearly, to conceptualize the intricacy of the process, a third term—encompassing the role of other actors in addition to Jews and Germans—was needed to move the discussion forward. It was once again Hilberg who came up with a felicitous suggestion. In 1992, he published *Perpetrators, Victims, Bystanders: The Jewish Catastrophe, 1933–1945*, and while the book's content did not generate overwhelming interest, its title—indeed, one word from the title—made a phenomenal career. "Bystanders" became a staple of Holocaust historiography's vocabulary, filling the need for the "third term," as it were.

With time, historians began to question the concept. What could it mean to be a "bystander" when confronted with radical violence to which the Jews during the Holocaust were subjected, especially in Eastern Europe? Is "standing by" a fitting characterization of what local people and institutions were mostly doing? Enough had by then been written about the contributions of the Vichy administration in France to the roundups and deportations of Jews, or the role of Hungarian gendarmerie in the summer 1944 mass deportation of Hungarian Jews to Auschwitz, or about the killings of Jews carried out by auxiliary police formations staffed by locals in the East, to induce a critical evaluation of the concept. Today, in tune with the earlier quoted passage from Friedländer and new monographs compiling supporting evidence, scholars would be inclined to recognize terms such as "implicated subjects," "facilitators" and/or "beneficiaries" as a far more apt characterizations of the contribution to the destruction of European Jews by the surrounding population.[8]

For me, the path to relying on personal testimonies when writing about the history of occupation in Eastern Europe during the Second World War opened fairly early. To start, I was trained as a historical sociologist, and the use of questionnaires, including open-ended survey data as well as personal accounts, is the staple of the profession.[9] In any case, since the release of Claude Lanzmann's *Shoah* in 1985, no one could doubt the significance of personal testimonies for understanding of the Holocaust. Simply put, during periods of social upheaval and disorganization—when institutions collapse and people's interactions are mostly unmediated by bureaucratic routines; when life of the community overflows regular channels, so to speak, and is no longer captured by institutional reporting—the best way, probably the only way, to record and understand what is taking place is through examination of personal testimonies. A casualty report after a riot may give an "objective" count of the number of corpses felled in the streets, but it will say precious little about what actually happened. Instead, "subjective," personal, testimonies offer an empirical foundation for making sense of what goes on in such circumstances. The Holocaust belongs to such a category of violent, unstructured, and fluid social phenomena, which can best be understood on the basis of evidence produced by myriad individual experiences put together.

In hindsight, it seems to me that *Neighbors'* contribution was both methodological (by providing a powerful valuation of personal testimonies for the study of the Holocaust) and substantive—by providing a composite description of an extremely violent episode of local people's complicity in the extermination of the Jews. This was a story of just one little town, but historians had already known for a long time about a wave of internecine violence that decimated Jewish communities in a swath of territory conquered by the Wehrmacht on the Eastern front in the summer of 1941. Readers understood the Jedwabne massacre as a *pars pro toto*. A composite image evoked in *Neighbors* by multiple voices of witnesses and participants gave concrete and memorable shape to the violence, which could be seen as a compilation of well-delineated actions—by specific, often named, individuals—rather than chaos. The immediately launched investigation of this mass murder by the Institute of National Memory (IPN) in Poland promptly identified some twenty other townships in the area where local, non-Jewish Poles killed their Jewish neighbors, on occasion even prior to the entry therein of German troops.[10]

Neighbors had originally been published in May 2000, in Polish, by a small printing house, Pogranicze (Borderlands). I appreciated the sensitivity of the subject and had not been sure whether a mainstream publisher would be ready to take the book.[11] I also wanted to place the manuscript in trusted hands. Krzysztof Czyżewski, the founder of the Borderlands Foundation, immediately recognized the book's significance and published it forthwith.[12] *Neighbors* did not initially have a wide distribution, and it took a good six months before the main daily newspaper, *Gazeta Wyborcza*, published an article about it. After that, it seemed as if floodgates had opened, and a long, wide-ranging public discussion began— perhaps, the most complex confrontation with collective memory, and the need to revise it, that the Poles had ever faced. Radio and television programs, newspaper articles and interviews, essays in professional journals produced between, roughly, November 2000 (when public discussion took off) and July 2001 (when sixtieth anniversary ceremonies to commemorate the mass murder were held) numbered in the thousands. A good sampling of voices articulating a spectrum of initial responses to *Neighbors* can be found in the 2003 volume *The Neighbors Respond: The Controversy over the Jedwabne Massacre in Poland*, edited by Antony Polonsky and Joanna Michlic.[13]

On July 9, 2002, Poland's Institute of National Memory issued what amounted to a final communiqué concerning its twenty-month investigation of the Jedwabne murder. "The findings," reported the *New York Times* on the following day, "which have been eagerly awaited in Poland, were a vindication for Mr. Gross."[14] Key elements of the book's narrative have been therein confirmed: the murder of Jedwabne Jews was planned in advance by local inhabitants, and many flocked into Jedwabne in the early morning hours of July 10 from outlying villages to take part in it;

direct involvement of the few Germans present on the scene was limited to assisting in the early phase of the crime, when Jews were assembled on the market square; individual killings were taking place all along, before the victims were walked to the barn and set on fire; all but a few dozen Jews present in Jedwabne on that day, including scores who sought refuge there from other towns, were killed; "executors of this crime, in the strict sense of the word, were Polish inhabitants of Jedwabne and vicinity—at least forty males"; property of murdered Jews was plundered after the killing.

The IPN worked under heavy pressure to prove the story of the Jedwabne murder wrong, or to fuzz the issue. But the impeccable integrity to public service of two officials—the prosecutor directly in charge of the investigation, Radosław Ignatiew, and the then head of the Institute of National Memory, Professor Leon Kieres—prevailed in the end.[15]

One element of the otherwise scrupulous and professional handling of the investigation was incompetent. The exhumation of the mass grave in Jedwabne, which should have taken many months to be carried out properly, was completed in five days in June 2001 with a removal of only topsoil covering the site. The procedure was cut short in deference to the demands of religious Jews in Poland and Israel, who were against disturbing the remains of the dead, but at least it allowed the IPN to identify remains of babies, small children, women, and elderly among the victims, and thus put an end to claims of right-wing apologists who implied that Jewish collaborators of Soviet secret police had been murdered in a revenge killing on July 10. Unfortunately, it was also the source of a hastily produced estimate of "300 to 400" victims allegedly being buried in the mass grave.

Needless to say, the character as well as the moral and historical implications of the Jedwabne mass murder remain exactly the same, no matter whether 400 people or 1,600 people were killed there. Yet because the IPN investigation established that all but a few dozen Jews had been murdered on that day, in order for the smaller number to make sense, one would have to account for some 1,000 Jews from Jedwabne and vicinity who were in town on July 10. In any event, IPN investigators evidently felt bound to accept the figures produced as a result of the incomplete forensic expertise they commissioned. Ironically, this is a point taken up now, entirely in bad faith, by extreme right-wing xenophobes who argue that the IPN investigation is inconclusive—indeed, wrong—and Poles would be exonerated had the exhumation not been interrupted in deference to Jewish religious law.

Two decades later, two divergent responses to the Jedwabne murder stand out. On one hand, there has been a truly extraordinary proliferation of scholarship and artistic production about all aspects of Polish-Jewish relations during the Second World War—a profound reckoning with the legacy of this "difficult past." Especially significant was the establishment in 2003 of the Polish Center for Holocaust Research (https://www.holocaustresearch.pl/?l=a&lang=en) at the Polish Academy of Sciences in Warsaw.[16] In addition, many scholars unaffiliated with the Center, publishing in periodicals from all the disciplines in the humanities, are also key contributors to this amazingly rich new field of research and writing. A good sampling in English of the current writings on the Holocaust in Poland, reflecting a variety of interests and approaches, can be found in a forthcoming volume, *Breaking the Frame*.[17]

Neighbors has given a push to the proliferation of this literature, but there was something in the air already, and it surfaced unexpectedly all over Eastern Europe. When Communism fell in the region—in the so-called miraculous year (*annus mirabilis*) 1989—and then the Soviet Union dissolved, local societies regained sovereignty and proceeded to freely organize their politics. They also, presumably, regained their pasts. Subjugated for decades under Communist Party censorship, people(s) were now free to study previously inaccessible state, secret police, and Communist Party archives in their respective countries. And when they did, it turned out that there were no real skeletons hidden in the closets as far as the period of the Communist rule was concerned: no big secrets unearthed; no as-yet unaired misdeeds of the Communists brought to the surface; nothing that would shed radically new light on significant episodes of contemporary history. At most, the opening of secret police archives led to little more than witch hunts, with personal reputations destroyed when it was revealed that some public figure had not owned up to the fact that he or she, at some point in the past, was a secret police collaborator.

Simultaneously, however, it began to surface in Eastern Europe that the "difficult past"—one that had not been "worked-through" or even narrated in accordance with the facts—was the Second World War and the German occupation of the region. One aspect in particular was blowing up the accepted clichés, which rooted the sense of collective identity of the locals in a narrative about the suffering and persecution experienced at the hands of the communists and/or the fascists: the untold story of complicity of the local population in the extermination of the Jews. This has been, it turned out, the real skeleton rattling in the closet of twentieth-century East European societies.

Not surprisingly, there was also a completely opposite reaction—a "backlash" (a brilliant Polish scholar called it)—emanating from the so-called patriotic, indeed nationalistic, segments of Polish society.[18] The backlash fed into stereotypes and prejudices of a large public entrenched in a traditional worldview promulgated by the Catholic Church.[19] Since

2015, following the electoral victory of the nationalistic and xenophobic Law and Justice Party (PiS), the pushback with respect to the Jedwabne massacre dominates government-controlled public life. One of the policies of the Law and Justice Party is especially relevant here—its so-called politics of history (*polityka historyczna*). Based on the premise that any government has a right to advocate a vision of its country's history that it likes, the *polityka historyczna* promoted by the current regime in Poland aims—as per official PiS slogans—to "raise Poland from its knees." No more "pedagogy of shame," PiS politicians and affiliated intellectuals proclaim in response to the wide-ranging discussion about Poles' co-responsibility for the persecution of their Jewish fellow citizens during the war. "Westerplatte [the site of heroic resistance against the German assault at the beginning of the war] or Jedwabne," a prominent historian rhetorically framed the alternative in an article published by a large circulation daily: a national community cannot be constituted on the basis of shame.[20]

What could perhaps evolve into an interesting discussion among educated professionals, when instrumentalized by politicians, turned into crass mendacity. For the past several years the PiS regime, through designated institutions, has advocated a false narrative that Polish society during the German occupation, for the most part, tried to save its Jewish fellow citizens. This is in contradiction to historical evidence, and the continuing work of the New Polish School of Holocaust Scholarship—internationally recognized for its professional excellence—provides mounting evidence to the contrary.[21] The regime has tried to gag further research in the field through legislation, intimidation, and propaganda.[22] Recently, in a bizarre incident of judicial overreach, two founders of the Polish Center for Holocaust Research, scholars with stellar international reputations, Professors Jan Grabowski and Barbara Engelking, were sentenced in February 2021 by a Warsaw court for "careless" interpretation of historical evidence.[23]

This is not meant to say that there weren't any Poles who tried to save their fellow Jewish citizens during the war. The Yad Vashem in Jerusalem recognized over seven thousand Poles as "Righteous among the Nations." So, there were Polish neighbors who had helped the Jews, and many lost their lives while doing so—primarily, because they were treated as pariahs in their own society. They were spied on and denounced to the Germans by their own neighbors. Long after the war had ended, they were afraid to admit to their noble deeds, fearing ostracism and even violence from their own community.[24] Irena Sendler, a courageous rescuer who saved many Jewish children, put it thus: "It is certain that it was much easier to find a place in a living room in occupied Warsaw where a large tank would be hidden under the carpet, than find a place for one little Jewish child."[25]

After three decades of research and writing about Poland's wartime history, the story of the Jedwabne mass murder caught me totally unprepared. To write *Neighbors* I needed to lift my own incredulity at what the evidence revealed. It took time and it came in stages, and this personal experience of only gradually coming to grips with what had happened gave me an understanding for the reluctance of the reading public in Poland to absorb the story. The manner in which mass murder in Jedwabne was carried out went against the grain of the national myth of victimization so central to Polish identity and rooted in the experience of so many Polish families. And yet, it turned out that this master narrative was not incompatible with numerous people acting out violently against another group of victims—the Jedwabne episode was only one among many acts of brutality against Jewish Poles carried out by non-Jewish Poles. But Jewish testimonies documenting this fact had been for a long time ignored. I was troubled by my own ignorance of this duality—where people may be victimized and act as victimizers at the same time—despite so many years of reading, research, and family conversations about the experience of war and occupation.[26]

The publication of *Neighbors* was a teachable moment about the ugliest face of Polish anti-Semitism, just as the murder of George Floyd was a teachable moment about institutionalized racist violence in America. A few years ago, I would have thought that the official backlash would not really matter in the face of accumulating historiography of the Shoah, which steadily compounds evidence of local people's complicity in the persecution of their Jewish fellow citizens. I was convinced, as I wrote in the afterword to the 2002 edition of *Neighbors*, that the next generations of Poles would learn the facts and soberly reflect on them and absorb their significance. But I am no longer so unequivocally optimistic.

The ascendancy of Trumpism in America and the way it lingers after the 2020 presidential election, in defiance of common sense, put everyone on notice that facts and sober reflection may not necessarily prevail in the public mind. It revealed also that racism, xenophobia, and mendacity in public life are not an exclusive prerogative of some faraway countries. "En Pologne c'est-a-dire nulle part" (In Poland, that is, nowhere), Alfred Jarry famously quipped in his surrealist play *Ubu Roi*. Except that Poland is not "nowhere," and neither is the United States. And even though mendacity flowing from the seats of government will not change history, I am afraid it will make writing honestly and learning about the past more of a challenge.

PARIS, JUNE–JULY 2021

1. My first book on the subject, *Polish Society under German Occupation: The Generalgouvernement, 1939–1944*, came out at Princeton University Press, in 1979; the next big monograph, *Revolution from Abroad: The Soviet Conquest of Poland's Western Ukraine and Western Belorussia*, was also published by Princeton, in 1988.

2. Saul Friedländer, *The Years of Extermination: Nazi Germany and the Jews, 1939–1945* (New York: HarperCollins, 2007), xxi (emphasis in the original).

3. Mark Mazower, *Hitler's Empire: How the Nazis Ruled Europe* (New York: Penguin Press, 2008), 6ff.

4. Ringelblum had been captured and killed in 1944, but miraculously most of the carefully hidden collection was recovered from the ruins of the Warsaw ghetto after the war and is now preserved in the Jewish Historical Institute in Warsaw as the Ringelblum Archive. The institute honored this pioneer of Holocaust studies by changing its name to Żydowski Instytut Historyczny imienia Emanuela Ringelbluma.

5. The most bloody episode in a series of anti-Semitic outbursts was the pogrom in the Polish city of Kielce on July 4, 1946, where forty-two people were killed. Afterward, Jewish emigration from Poland spiked, and over one hundred thousand people fled the country within a few months.

6. Mordechaj Canin, *Przez ruiny i zgliszcza* [Through ruins and destruction] (Warsaw: Nisza, 2019).

7. The work of compiling personal documentation of the Holocaust went on in many places. Numerous archival collections around the world are holding and preserving the data—the best-known and the most comprehensive being the Yad Vashem in Jerusalem and the US Holocaust Memorial Museum in Washington, DC. And the work will continue for as long as any Holocaust survivors are

still alive, under the auspices of the Visual History Archive sponsored by the University of Southern California's Shoah Foundation in Los Angeles.

8. I encountered the terms in Mary Fulbrook's excellent monograph *A Small Town near Auschwitz: Ordinary Nazis and the Holocaust* (Oxford: Oxford University Press, 2012); see also Michael Rothberg, *The Implicated Subject: Beyond Victims and Perpetrators* (Stanford, CA: Stanford University Press, 2019).

9. My early work with "ego documents," as they are called in the profession, on the social history of the Second World War followed an accidental discovery in the archives of the Hoover Institution on War, Revolution, and Peace at Stanford University. I found there a trove of handwritten statements describing people's experiences under the Soviet occupation of the eastern half of Poland between 1939 and 1941. In the 1980s, I published two volumes of documents (together with Irena Grudzińska-Gross) and wrote a book-length monograph about the way Soviet power was introduced in the conquered territories—*Revolution from Abroad: The Soviet Conquest of Poland's Western Ukraine and Western Belorussia*.

10. Paweł Machcewicz and Krzysztof Persak, eds., *Wokół Jedwabnego* [Concerning Jedwabne], 2 vols. (Warsaw: Instytut Pamięci Narodowej, 2002). This is an invaluable—more than 1,500 pages—compilation of archival sources (vol. 1) and scholarly essays (vol. 2) on issues related to the Jedwabne mass murder and other similar episodes in the surrounding territory of the Białystok voivodeship. See, in particular, the introduction by Persak and Machcewicz.

11. Henryk Woźniakowski, the editor of Znak, who later published two of my books on the subject of Polish-Jewish relationships—*Fear: Anti-Semitism in Poland after*

Auschwitz (Kraków: Znak, 2008), and *The Golden Harvest* (with Irena Grudzińska-Gross) (Kraków: Znak, 2011)—in his latest book recalls when I told him that I was working on the Jedwabne murder. He took our conversation, he says, as a sounding out whether Znak would be interested in the manuscript. At the time, he writes, he dropped the subject: "I decided, that we were not ready for this" (Woźniakowski, *Rzeczy ważne a czasem błahe* [Matters of importance and also trivia] Krakow: Znak, 2021, 296).

12. Krzysztof Czyżewski is a well-known essayist and cultural organizer promoting cross-cultural dialogue in Eastern Europe through his Borderlands Foundation.

13. (Princeton, NJ: Princeton University Press, 2003).

14. To be sure, I needed vindication only from my detractors, but they remained impervious to rational arguments or evidence and merely changed the target of their attacks from *Neighbors* to IPN.

15. See the newspaper *Rzeczpospolita*, July 10, 2002. For his determination and fairness throughout the whole process Kieres and his family received hate mail and anonymous calls ("The Worst Letters Are Kept away from Me," was the title of a long interview he gave for *Gazeta Wyborcza's Magazine* on July 5, 2001), and he was verbally abused in the parliament by right-wing deputies, one of them calling on Kieres to resign so that "a real Pole" could be appointed to his job.

16. Since 2005, the Center publishes thick, yearly journals of close to one thousand pages each, titled *Holocaust Studies and Materials* (*Zagłada Żydów: Studia i Materiały*). The content of the sixteen volumes published so far, together with numerous monographs that the Center puts out under its imprint, constitute the backbone of what may be called the "New Polish School of Holocaust Scholarship."

17. Irena Grudzińska Gross and Konrad Maty-

jaszek, eds., *Breaking the Frame: New School of Polish-Jewish Studies* (Frankfurt: Peter Lang, 2021).

18. Piotr Forecki, *Po Jedwabnem: Anatomia pamięci funkcjonalnej* [After Jedwabne: Anatomy of functional memory] (Warsaw: IBL, 2018).

19. A particularly influential brand of Catholicism under the current political regime in Poland is represented by a Redemptorist priest, Father Rydzyk, and his media empire. He is lionized by the political elite of the Law and Justice Party, and generously funded in his assorted initiatives from the government budget. In 2008, in an official US publication titled *Contemporary Global Anti-Semitism: A Report Provided to the United States Congress*, Rydzyk's broadcasting station, Radio Maryja, was characterized as "one of Europe's most blatantly anti-Semitic media venues" (US Department of State, *Contemporary Global Anti-Semitism*, chap. 6).

20. Forecki, *Po Jedwabnem*, 38, 39.

21. An international conference honoring the achievements of Polish scholars organized by a leading university in Paris in February 2019—the Ecole des Hautes Etudes en Sciences Sociales—provided a shocking spectacle to French academics when a posse of PiS regime sympathizers staged their vocal anti-Semitic protests. Several articles have been written about this episode in France. The event's notoriety prompted the drafting of an informative Wikipedia entry, "New Polish School of Holocaust Scholarship (conference)," which contains also a good bibliography.

I may add that an earlier conference where scholars from the Polish Center of Holocaust Research discussed their findings with American colleagues—The Holocaust in Poland: New Findings and New Interpretations (Princeton, NJ, October 2010)—also triggered an unprofessional response from the Polish consul general in New York, which shocked American scholars (see Benjamin Frommer, "Postscript: The Holocaust in Occupied Poland, Then and Now," *East European Politics and Societies* 25, no. 3, 2011, 575–80).

22. The legislative attempt, which created an uproar of international protests, particularly from Israel and the United States, was a January 2018 law that stated "whoever publicly, and without factual base, accuses the Polish nation, or the Polish state, of responsibility for the Nazi crimes committed by the III German Reich, or other crimes against humanity, against peace and other war crimes, will be subject to a prison term of up to three years and/or a fine." It was widely recognized as an attempt to discourage research on Polish complicity in the persecution of Jews during the German occupation. It also criminalized personal experiences of all those Jews who had ever been extorted, blackmailed, or denounced by the Poles—as most survivors had been at some point. Now, if they spoke about it, they would be violating Polish law.

23. On August 16, 2021, the Appeals Court in Warsaw decisively overturned the conviction stating, among other things, that courts have no business to interfere with scientific research, that the lower court's verdict was tantamount to imposition of censorship, and that in the history of every country there are difficult periods, which must be confronted through public discussion. For details, see Jan Grabowski's article about the trial in Gross and Matyjaszek, *Breaking the Frame*.

24. For specific examples, see my introduction to *Fear: Anti-Semitism in Poland after Auschwitz*.

25. Anna Bikont, *Sendlerowa: W ukryciu* [Mrs. Sendler. In hiding] (Wołowiec: Czarne, 2017, 339).

26. I wrote a chapter titled "Blinded by Social Distance," reflecting on the inability to recognize the extent of anti-Jewish violence by the Poles in *Fear: Anti-Semitism in Poland after Auschwitz* (New York: Random House, 2006).

ACKNOWLEDGMENTS

This book could not have been written without the assistance of Rabbi Jacob Baker in New York and Professor Andrzej Paczkowski in Warsaw. I gratefully acknowledge Rabbi Baker's permission to reproduce the photographs included here. I am grateful to attorney Ty Rogers for putting me in touch with many former Jedwabne residents and their descendants.

I owe a debt of gratitude to several people who helped me with the writing of this book. For the most part I thank them in the endnotes. Here, I would like to express my special thanks to Stephanie Steiker for her editorial assistance and unfailing emotional support, as well as to Valerie Steiker and Magda Gross for many useful editorial suggestions. I am deeply grateful to Lauren Lepow for copyediting the final draft of the manuscript with consummate skill.

I wish to thank the Remarque Institute of New York University for appointing me a faculty fellow in spring 2000. This provided me with ample time to complete the manuscript. The Institute's director, Tony Judt, as well as two readers for Princeton University Press, Mark Mazower and Antony Polonsky, offered useful comments for which I am also grateful. Last but not least, I want to thank the history editor at Princeton University Press, Brigitta van Rheinberg, who watched over the manuscript of this book with skill and enthusiasm from the beginning.

I dedicate *Neighbors* to the memory of Szmul Wasersztajn.

NEW YORK
JUNE 2000

NEIGHBORS

INTRODUCTION

Twentieth-century Europe has been shaped decisively by the actions of two men. It is to Adolf Hitler and Joseph Stalin that we owe totalitarianism—if not its invention, then certainly its most determined implementation. The loss of life for which they are jointly responsible is truly staggering. Yet it is not what happened but what has been prevented from ever taking place that gives a truer measure of totalitarianism's destructiveness: "the sum of unwritten books," as one author put it. In fact, the sum of thoughts unthought, of unfelt feelings, of works never accomplished, of lives unlived to their natural end.[1]

Not only the goals but also the methods of totalitarian politics crippled societies where they were deployed, and among the most gripping was the institutionalization of resentment. People subject to Stalin's or Hitler's rule were repeatedly set against each other and encouraged to act on the basest instincts of mutual dislike. Every conceivable cleavage in society was eventually exploited, every antagonism exacerbated. At one time or another city was set against the countryside, workers against peasants, middle peasants against poor peasants, children against their parents, young against old, and ethnic groups against each other. Secret police encouraged, and thrived on, denunciations: *divide et impera* writ large. In addition, as social mobilization and mass participation in state-sponsored institutions and rituals were required, people became, to varying degrees, complicitous in their own subjugation.

Totalitarian rulers also imposed a novel pattern of occupation in the territories they conquered. As a result, wrote Hannah Arendt, "they who were the Nazis' first accomplices and their best aides truly did not know what they were doing nor with whom they were dealing."[2] It turned out that there was no adequate word in European languages to define this relationship. The term "collaboration"—in its specific connotation of a morally objectionable association with an enemy—came into usage only in the context of the Second World War.[3] Given that armed conflicts, conquests, wars, occupations, subjugations, territorial expansions, and their accompanying circumstances are as old as recorded human history, one wonders what novelty in the phenomenon of German occupation during the Second World War stimulated the emergence of a fresh concept.[4] Was it the Holocaust, or should a comprehensive answer to this question be sought in multiple studies of German regimes of occupation?

After the fact, public opinion all over Europe recoiled in disgust at virtually any form of engagement with the Nazis (in an arguably somewhat self-serving and not always sincere reaction). "It is nearly impossible to calculate the total number of persons targeted by postwar retribution, but, even by the most conservative estimates, they numbered several million, that is 2 or 3 percent of the population formerly under German occupation," writes

Istvan Deák in a recent study. "Punishments of the guilty ranged from lynchings during the last months of the war to postwar death sentencing, imprisonment, or hard labor. Added to those harsh punishments were condemnation to national dishonor, the loss of civic rights, and/or monetary fines as well as such administrative measures as expulsions, police supervision, loss of the right to travel or to live in certain desirable places, dismissal, and the loss of pension rights."[5] "This was a war," to quote Heda Kovaly's poignant memoir from Prague, "that no one had quite survived."[6]

While the experience of the Second World War has to a large extent shaped the political makeup and destinies of all European societies in the second half of the twentieth century, Poland has been singularly affected. It was over the territory of the pre-1939 Polish state that Hitler and Stalin first joined in a common effort (their pact of nonaggression signed in August 1939 included a secret clause dividing the country in half) and then fought a bitter war until one of them was eventually destroyed. As a result Poland suffered a demographic catastrophe without precedent; close to 20 percent of its population died of war-related causes. It lost its minorities—Jews in the Holocaust, and Ukrainians and Germans following border shifts and population movements after the war. Poland's elites in all walks of life were decimated. Over a third of its urban residents were missing at the conclusion of the war. Fifty-five percent of the country's lawyers were no more, along with 40 percent of its medical doctors and one-third of its university professors and Roman Catholic clergy.[7] Poland was dubbed "God's playground" by a sympathetic British historian,[8] but during that time it must have felt more like a stomping ground of the devil.

The centerpiece of the story I am about to present in this little volume falls, to my mind, utterly out of scale: one day, in July 1941, half of the population of a small East European town murdered the other half—some 1,600 men, women, and children. Consequently, in what follows, I will discuss the Jedwabne murders in the context of numerous themes invoked by the phrase "Polish-Jewish relations during the Second World War."[9]

First and foremost I consider this volume a challenge to standard historiography of the

Second World War, which posits that there are two separate wartime histories—one pertaining to the Jews and the other to all the other citizens of a given European country subjected to Nazi rule. This is a particularly untenable position with respect to Poland's history of those years, given the size of, and social space occupied by, Polish Jewry. On the eve of the war, Poland's was the second largest agglomeration of Jews in the world, after the American Jewry. About 10 percent of prewar Polish citizens identified themselves—either by Mosaic faith or by declaring Yiddish to be their mother tongue—as Jews. Nearly one-third of the Polish urban population was Jewish. And yet the Holocaust of Polish Jews has been bracketed by historians as a distinct, separate subject that only tangentially affects the rest of Polish society. Conventional wisdom maintains that only "socially marginal" individuals in Polish society—the so-called *szmalcownicy*,[10] or "scum," who blackmailed Jews, and the heroes who lent them a helping hand—were involved with the Jews.

This is not the place to argue in detail why such views are untenable. Perhaps it is not even necessary to dwell at length on this matter. After all, *how can the wiping out of one-third of its urban population be anything other than a central issue of Poland's modern history?* In any case, one certainly needs no great methodological sophistication to grasp instantly that when the Polish half of a town's population murders its Jewish half, we have on our hands an event patently invalidating the view that these two ethnic groups' histories are disengaged.

The second point that readers of this volume must keep in mind is that Polish-Jewish relations during the war are conceived in a standard analysis as mediated by outside forces—the Nazis and the Soviets. This, of course, is correct as far as it goes. The Nazis and the Soviets were indeed calling the shots in the Polish territories they occupied during the war. But one should not deny the reality of autonomous dynamics in the relationships between Poles and Jews within the constraints imposed by the occupiers. There were things people could have done at the time and refrained from doing; and there were things they did not have to do but nevertheless did. Ac-

cordingly, I will be particularly careful to identify who did what in the town of Jedwabne on
July 10, 1941, and at whose behest.

In August 1939, as is well known, Hitler
and Stalin concluded a pact of nonaggression.
Its secret clauses demarcated the boundaries
of influence spheres between the two dictators
in Central Europe. One month later the territory of Poland was carved out between the
Third Reich and the USSR. The town of Jedwabne first found itself in the Soviet zone of
occupation and later, after Hitler attacked the
Soviet Union, was taken over by the Nazis. An
important issue I thus felt compelled to address concerns the standard historiographical
perspective on Soviet-Jewish relations during
the twenty-month-long Soviet rule over the
half of Poland the Red Army occupied starting
in September 1939. Again this is not the place
to put the matter to rest.[11] We will simply have
to remember that according to the current stereotype Jews enjoyed a privileged relationship
with the Soviet occupiers. Allegedly the Jews
collaborated with the Soviets at the expense of
the Poles, and therefore an outburst of brutal
Polish antisemitism, at the time the Nazis invaded the USSR, may have come in the terri-

tories liberated from under Bolshevik rule in 1941 as a response to this experience. I therefore explore whether there were any linkages between what happened in Jedwabne under the Soviet occupation (September 1939–June 1941) and immediately thereafter.

The Jedwabne massacre touches upon yet another historiographical topos concerning this epoch—one maintaining that Jews and communism were bound by a mutually beneficial relationship. Hence, allegedly, the presence of antisemitism among broad strata of Polish society (or any other East European society, for that matter) after the war, and the special role Jews played in establishing and consolidating Stalinism in Eastern Europe. I will address this issue briefly in the discussion of my study's sources and will return to these and related matters in the concluding chapters.

As to the broader context of Holocaust studies, this book cannot be easily located on the functionalist–intentionalist spectrum. It stands askew of this distinction, already blurred in recent Holocaust historiography, and belongs instead to a genre—"only now beginning to receive appropriate scholarly attention"—that belabors the "pepetrators-victims-bystanders" axis.[12] But it shows that these terms are also fuzzy and can be read as a reminder that each episode of mass killing had its own situational dynamics. This is not a trivial point, for it means—and further studies will, I think, demonstrate that Jedwabne was not unique in this respect—that in each episode many specific individual decisions were made by different actors present on the scene, who decisively influenced outcomes. And, thus, it is at least conceivable that a number of those actors could have made different choices, with the result that many more European Jews could have survived the war.

In an important respect, however, this is a rather typical book about the Holocaust. For, as is not true of historical studies we write about other topics, I do not see the possibility of attaining closure here. In other words, the reader will not emerge with a sense of satisfied yearning for knowledge at the conclusion of reading; I certainly did not do so at the conclusion of writing. I could not say to myself when I got to the last page, "Well, I understand now," and I doubt that my readers will be able to either.

Of course one must proceed with the exposition and analysis *as if* it were possible to understand, and address prevailing interpretive historiographical strands. But I think it is in the nature of the subject matter that we will have to pose queries at the end of the story—and how about this? and how about that? And this is just as well, since perhaps the only relief we may hope to find when confronted with the Holocaust is in the process of asking such endless follow-up questions, to which we will continue to look for answers. The Holocaust thus stands at a point of departure rather than a point of arrival in humankind's ceaseless efforts to draw lessons from its own experience. And while we will never "understand" why it happened, we must clearly understand the implications of its having taken place. In this sense it becomes a foundational event of modern sensibility, forever afterward to be an essential consideration in reflections about the human condition.

OUTLINE OF THE STORY

On January 8, 1949, in the small town of Jedwabne, some nineteen kilometers from Łomża in Poland's historical province of Mazowsze, security police detained fifteen men. We find their names in a memorandum ominously called *Raport likwidacyjny* (A liquidation report) among the so-called control-investigative files (*akta kontrolno-śledcze*) kept by the security police to monitor their own progress in each investigation.[1] Among the arrested, mostly small farmers and seasonal workers, there were two shoemakers, a mason, a carpenter, two locksmiths, a letter carrier, and a former town-hall receptionist. Some were family men (one a father of six children, another of four), some still unattached. The youngest was twenty-seven years old, the oldest sixty-four. They were, to put it simply, a bunch of ordinary men.[2]

Jedwabne's inhabitants, at the time totaling about two thousand, must have been shocked by the simultaneous arrests of so many local residents.[3] The wider public got a glimpse of the whole affair four months later, when, on May 16 and 17 in the District Court of Łomża, Bolesław Ramotowski and twenty-one codefendants were put on trial. The opening sentence of the indictment reads, "Jewish Historical Institute in Poland sent materials to the Ministry of Justice describing criminal activities of the inhabitants of Jedwabne who engaged in the murder of Jewish people, as stated in the testimony of Szmul Wasersztajn who witnessed the pogrom of the Jews."[4]

There are no records at the Jewish Historical Institute (JHI) telling us how or when Wasersztajn's deposition was communicated to the prosecutor's office. On the basis of the court files, likewise, it is impossible to know, for example, when the prosecution was informed about what had happened in Jedwabne, and why the indictment was so long delayed. The control-investigative files from the Łomża Security Office shed some light on the matter, but they are also inconclusive.[5] In any case, Wasersztajn gave his testimony before the Jewish Historical Commission in Białystok on April 5, 1945. And this is what he said:

Before the war broke out, 1,600 Jews lived in Jedwabne, and only seven survived, saved by a Polish woman, Wyrzykowska, who lived in the vicinity.

On Monday evening, June 23, 1941, Germans entered the town. And as early as the 25th local bandits, from the Polish population, started an anti-Jewish pogrom. Two of those bandits, Borowski (Borowiuk?) Wacek with his brother Mietek, walked from one Jewish dwelling to another together with other bandits playing accordion and flute to drown the screams of Jewish women and children. I saw with my own eyes how those murderers killed Chajcia Wasersztajn, Jakub Kac, seventy-three years old, and Eliasz Krawiecki.

Jakub Kac they stoned to death with bricks. Krawiecki they knifed and then plucked his eyes and cut off his tongue. He suffered terribly for twelve hours before he gave up his soul.

On the same day I observed a horrible scene. Chaja Kubrzańska, twenty-eight years old, and Basia Binsztajn, twenty-six years old, both holding newborn babies, when they saw what was going on, they ran to a pond, in order to drown themselves with the children rather than fall into the hands of bandits. They put their children in the water and drowned them with their own hands: then Baśka Binsztajn jumped in and immediately went to the bottom, while Chaja Kubrzańska suffered for a couple of hours. Assembled hooligans made a spectacle of this. They advised her to lie face down in the water, so that she would drown faster. Finally, seeing that the children were already dead, she threw herself more energetically into the water and found her death too.

The next day a local priest intervened, explaining that they should stop the pogrom, and that German authorities would take care of things by themselves. This worked, and the pogrom was stopped. From this day on the local population no longer sold foodstuffs to Jews, which made their circumstances all the more difficult. In the meantime rumors spread that the Germans would issue an order that all the Jews be destroyed.

Such an order was issued by the Germans on
July 10, 1941.

Even though the Germans gave the order, it
was Polish hooligans who took it up and carried
it out, using the most horrible methods. After various tortures and humiliations, they burned all
the Jews in a barn. During the first pogrom and
the later bloodbath the following outcasts distinguished themselves by their brutality: Szleziński,
Karolak, Borowiuk (Borowski?) Mietek, Borowiuk (Borowski?) Wacław, Jermałowski, Ramutowski Bolek, Rogalski Bolek, Szelawa Stanisław,
Szelawa Franciszek, Kozłowski Geniek, Trzaska,
Tarnoczek Jerzyk, Ludański Jurek, Laciecz
Czesław.

On the morning of July 10, 1941, eight gestapo men came to town and had a meeting with
representatives of the town authorities. When the
gestapo asked what their plans were with respect
to the Jews, they said, unanimously, that all Jews
must be killed. When the Germans proposed to
leave one Jewish family from each profession,
local carpenter Bronisław Szleziński, who was
present, answered: We have enough of our own
craftsmen, we have to destroy all the Jews, none
should stay alive. Mayor Karolak and everybody
else agreed with his words. For this purpose Szle-

ziński gave his own barn, which stood nearby. After this meeting the bloodbath began.

Local hooligans armed themselves with axes, special clubs studded with nails, and other instruments of torture and destruction and chased all the Jews into the street. As the first victims of their devilish instincts they selected seventy-five of the youngest and healthiest Jews, whom they ordered to pick up a huge monument of Lenin that the Russians had erected in the center of town. It was impossibly heavy, but under a rain of horrible blows the Jews had to do it. While carrying the monument, they also had to sing until they brought it to the designated place. There, they were ordered to dig a hole and throw the monument in. Then these Jews were butchered to death and thrown into the same hole.

The other brutality was when the murderers ordered every Jew to dig a hole and bury all previously murdered Jews, and then those were killed and in turn buried by others. It is impossible to represent all the brutalities of the hooligans, and it is difficult to find in our history of suffering something similar.

Beards of old Jews were burned, newborn babies were killed at their mothers' breasts, people were beaten murderously and forced to sing and

dance. In the end they proceeded to the main ac-
tion—the burning. The entire town was sur-
rounded by guards so that nobody could escape;
then Jews were ordered to line up in a column,
four in a row, and the ninety-year-old rabbi and
the shochet [Kosher butcher] *were put in front,*
they were given a red banner, and all were or-
dered to sing and were chased into the barn.
Hooligans bestially beat them up on the way.
Near the gate a few hooligans were standing,
playing various instruments in order to drown
the screams of horrified victims. Some tried to de-
fend themselves, but they were defenseless. Blood-
ied and wounded, they were pushed into the barn.
Then the barn was doused with kerosene and lit,
and the bandits went around to search Jewish
homes, to look for the remaining sick and chil-
dren. The sick people they found they carried to
the barn themselves, and as for the little children,
they roped a few together by their legs and car-
ried them on their backs, then put them on pitch-
forks and threw them onto smoldering coals.

After the fire they used axes to knock golden
teeth from still not entirely decomposed bodies
and in other ways violated the corpses of holy
martyrs.[6]

While it is clear to a reader of Wasersztajn's deposition that Jews were annihilated in Jedwabne with particular cruelty, it is difficult at first to fully absorb the meaning of his testimony. And, in a way, I am not at all surprised that four years had elapsed between the time when he made his statement and the beginning of the Łomża trial. This is, more or less, the amount of time that elapsed between my discovery of Wasersztajn's testimony in JHI's archives and my grasp of its factuality. When in the autumn of 1998 I was asked to contribute an article to a Festschrift prepared for Professor Tomasz Strzembosz—a well-known historian who specialized in wartime history of the Białystok region—I decided to use the example of Jedwabne to describe how Polish neighbors mistreated their Jewish cocitizens. But I did not fully register then that after the series of killings and cruelties described by Wasersztajn, at the end of the day *all* the remaining Jews were actually burned alive in a barn (I must have read this as a hyperbolic trope, concluding that only some had been killed that way). A few months after I submitted my essay, I watched raw footage for the documentary film *Where Is My Older Brother Cain?* made by Agnieszka Arnold, who, among other interlocutors, spoke with the daughter of Bronisław Śleszyński, and I realized that Wasersztajn has to be taken literally.

As the book had not yet been published, I wondered whether I should withdraw my chapter. However, I decided to leave the chapter unchanged, because one important aspect of the Jedwabne story concerns the slow dawning of Polish awareness of this horrendous crime. How did this event figure (or, rather, fail to figure) in the consciousness of historians of the war period—myself included? How did the population of Jedwabne live for three generations with the knowledge of these murders? How will the Polish citizenry process the revelation when it becomes public knowledge?[7]

In any case, once we realize that what seems inconceivable is precisely what happened, a historian soon discovers that the whole story is very well documented, that witnesses are still alive, and that the memory of this crime has been preserved in Jedwabne through the generations.

SOURCES

The best sources for a historian are those that provide a contemporaneous account of the events under scrutiny. My first step, therefore, was to seek German documentation of the destruction of Jews in this territory. Such documentation may exist somewhere, but I was not able to find it. Various scholars of the period whom I queried were unfamiliar with the place-name Jedwabne. In the daily summary reports of the *Einsatzgruppen*'s activities from the Eastern Front, where such information would have been included, Jedwabne is not mentioned. This is not surprising, since *Einsatzgruppe* B, which would earlier have been active in the Łomża area, on July 10 was already in the vicinity of Minsk.[1] But, with luck, we may yet be able to find German documentary footage shot at the time of the pogrom.[2]

As things stand, the first and the most comprehensive report about the Jedwabne massacre was filed by Szmul Wasersztajn in 1945. Then, we have evidence that was recorded during the Łomża trials in May 1949 and November 1953. In 1980 a memorial book of Jedwabne Jews was published, and in it several eyewitnesses described the tragedy of their hometown. In 1998 the filmmaker Agnieszka Arnold interviewed several town inhabitants on the subject. And later still, I had an opportunity to talk about these events with several former residents.[3] These are the main sources for this study, and before we grapple with the subject, a few observations on the proper use of these sources are in order.

First, we need a reminder that Jewish testimonies about the Shoah have been deliberately written down in order to provide an exact and comprehensive account of the catastrophe. This is evidenced in the numerous memoirs and journals kept by Jews at the time, as if the apocryphal exhortation of the great historian Simon Dubnow, before his deportation from Riga, calling on his fellow Jews "to write it all down" truly resounded in the hearts and minds of Jewish memoirists. The same intention informed collective efforts, which we know very well and revere for their scrupulous and ingenious attempt at recording and generating evidence—I have in mind the *Oneg Shabbat* initiative by Emanuel Ringelblum in the Warsaw ghetto, or the daunting work of archivists from the ghetto in Kovno.[4] Since it appeared impossible to save the Jewish people who were being methodically annihilated by the Nazi-organized killing process, a sense of obligation grew among Jewish record-keepers (they say so explicitly and repeatedly) that they must at least preserve the evidence of the very process of destruction.

We should read in these efforts an intuition that one could effectively oppose, indeed frustrate, the Nazis' plan of annihilation of the Jews if only a record of the Nazis' evil deeds was preserved. Victims of Nazi crimes apparently believed that engraving the whole story in memory and preserving it for posterity effectively cancelled the very essence of the Nazi project. *And there were no reasons whatsoever for*

Jews, in their recollection of Shoah episodes they experienced and witnessed, to attribute to Poles those crimes that were in reality perpetrated by the Germans. Every witness, of course, can make mistakes; and every story needs to be checked, if at all possible, against other stories. But Jewish witnesses to the Jedwabne massacre would not have falsified their accounts out of ill will vis-à-vis their Polish neighbors.

The bulk of documentation for this study comes not from Jewish victims, however, but from the perpetrators and was produced during a court trial. Dealing with such materials, we ought to appreciate in the first place that people suspected of wrongdoing might wish, as far as possible, to play down their own role in the events under scrutiny. They might also wish to trivialize the events themselves. We must keep in mind that the accused are not obliged, under the law, to reveal the truth in their depositions; while witnesses, even though sworn to tell the truth and nothing but the truth, can be selective in what they remember and terse in answering questions. Furthermore, between the source of evidence (a witness or an accused) and what is compiled in a document that a historian takes in hand, there is a mediating person (and in that sense a protocol of investigation is unlike a diary or a memoir, which puts the reader in direct communication with the source)—an investigator, a judge, a defense attorney, or a prosecutor, who structured and produced the document—who may be more or less intelligent, informed, or committed to finding the truth. Therefore, the quality of evidence garnered from trial materials will, for a historian, very much depend on the intentions and thoroughness of the investigation and the manner in which the trial itself was conducted.

Even a quick perusal of the court case against Ramotowski and his accomplices reveals that their trial was hastily organized. This may even be too kind a characterization, given that court proceedings against the twenty-two accused were completed within one day: the trial opened on May 16th, 1949, in the Łomża District Court, and on the next day sentences were handed down. Eight of the accused were found not guilty. Józef Sobuta, who was put on trial in 1953, was also set free.[5]

Critical appraisal of the sources depends on an awareness of such details, because both

1949 and 1953 were years of deep Stalinism in Poland. The judiciary as well as the investigative authorities (the so-called Security Office, *Urząd Bezpieczeństwa* [UB]) acquired in those years a well-deserved notoriety. Furthermore, in the courtroom defendants revealed that they were beaten during interrogation and thus compelled to make depositions—a very plausible complaint, given the methods that were employed at the time by the UB.

My supposition—given the way this entire investigation was handled—is that such treatment was bestowed on pretty much everyone brought during those years to the Łomża Security Office. In any case, there is no trace in this trial of efforts to elicit from the accused any specific information or to establish the existence of some conspiracy or clandestine organization linking them all together. A sudden amnesia during the trial, when the accused could not recall many of the fine points that they had revealed during interrogation, seems much less persuasive than their earlier ability to speak in considerable detail about the events of July 10.[6] We know, after all, that the circumstances of the July murders of Jedwabne Jews were a recurrent topic of conversation in town for years after the killing.

Reviewing all the materials assembled during the investigation for the Ramotowski trial, one soon realizes that the twenty-two accused were, with only a few exceptions, each deposed once. Protocols of depositions are brief and are framed around the same three questions: Where did you live in July 1941? Did you participate in the murder of Jews in the month of July? Who else participated in murdering and rounding up the Jews of Jedwabne? The bulk of these depositions is recorded in the same handwriting and signed by the same investigating official, Grzegorz Matujewicz. Except for a few supplementary protocols, they were mostly produced between the 8th and the 22d of January. In other words, the entire investigation was, in effect, carried out within a period of two weeks. We can conclude on this basis, it seems to me, that this was not a high-priority case for the Łomża Security Office, and that relatively little effort was put into it.

Quite indicative of the perfunctoriness with which the case was handled is the very phrasing of the act of accusation against Ramotowski and his accomplices. They were accused, we learn from the document, of having "acted in a manner that fostered the interests of the German state, by participating in the apprehension of some 1,200 people of Jewish nationality on June 25, 1941, in the town of Jedwabne in Łomża County, where the said people were burned by the Germans in a barn belonging to Bronisław Śleszyński."[7] Now, the Jedwabne mass murder of Jews took place on July 10th, and this fact is reflected in numerous depositions assembled during the investigation. But, clearly, what stuck in the prosecutor's mind was the first date, June 25th, mentioned in Wasersztajn's testimony. And for many months neither the prosecutor's office nor the court bothered to correct the mistake. Only in the judgment passed after the final appeal was filed before the Supreme Court do we find a clarification that "the Jedwabne murder took place a few days later than recognized by the District Court"—in fact, over two weeks later![8]

I present all this information, peripheral to the substance of the case, in order to establish beyond a reasonable doubt that this was not a political trial. Indeed, the content of the control-investigative files, which reflect the thinking and plans of the Security Office, confirms this assessment. In the "Liquidation Report" of January 24, 1949, previously quoted, rubric no. 5 reads, "Plan of Future Operational Activities." Nothing of special significance is noted therein. From this document, as well as from all the rest of the control-investigative files, it is evident that the matter was handled as a routine case. The late forties and early fifties, after all, were a time when Stalin's anti-Jewish phobia was at its peak and already serving as a driving force for political persecution throughout the entire camp of the so-called people's democracies.[9] Evidently, it was in no one's interest in Stalinist Poland to underscore Jewish wartime suffering at the hands of the Poles.

The case against Ramotowski had to be brought, I gather, because a complaint had been filed and had worked its way through the administrative machinery of the judicial system. But the matter was given short shrift in every respect and was disposed of as quickly as possible. And, for the very reason that this was

by no means a political trial, materials produced during the investigation can serve us
well in our reconstruction of what actually
took place, though we must not lose sight of
the fact that the accused are likely to have tried
to minimize both the events themselves and
the extent of their own involvement.[10]

BEFORE THE WAR

Jedwabne is situated at the intersection of two river valleys. The Narew and Biebrza Rivers overflow each spring, and the area is famous for picturesque swamps with untold varieties of waterfowl and lush vegetation. In 1979 the largest national park in Poland was established in the area.[1] But the town itself, irrespective of its beautiful surroundings, is ugly.

From time immemorial wood and straw have been the cheapest and most readily available construction materials in this part of the country, and fires have therefore plagued local inhabitants. The most devastating in people's memory consumed almost three-quarters of the town in 1916. Jedwabne's exceptionally beautiful eighteenth-century wooden synagogue had burned down three years earlier, before the outbreak of the First World War.[2] Writing for the memorial book of Jedwabne Jewry, one of the inhabitants recalled many decades later how each evening before going to sleep, people would cast a last glance toward the north, where just beyond the horizon lay the neighboring town of Radziłów. And if the night sky scintillated with a faint pink glow, they would promptly load wagons full of necessities and rush to the rescue. Similarly, the Radziłów Jews kept an eye on Jedwabne. Fires were frequent, and inhabitants of neighboring villages, often kinsfolk, shared both a common fate and their limited resources.

Jedwabne received its town charter in 1736, though at that time it had already been settled for at least three hundred years. Jews had come to Jedwabne from Tykocin (Tiktin) and were initially subject to the Tykocin Jewish communal authority. In 1770, when the beautiful wooden synagogue was built in Jedwabne, 387 Jews lived there, a substantial majority of the total population of 450. On the eve of the First World War the population of Jedwabne reached its all-time peak, approximating 3,000. Shortly thereafter, in 1916, their number shrunk to some 700 as a result of wartime devastation and the deliberate Russian policy of resettlement of Jews (who were suspected of pro–Central Powers sympathies) from territories immediately adjacent to the front line.

After the war a majority of the resettled returned, and the town began to recuperate. According to census figures of 1931, the town population then totaled 2,167, and over 60 percent of the inhabitants identified themselves as Jews. The remainder of the town population, as well as residents of the surrounding rural *gmina* (the smallest territorial unit of administration), were of Polish ethnicity.

In 1933 there were 144 craftsmen officially registered in Jedwabne, including 36 tailors and 24 shoemakers. Services and crafts were mostly Jewish occupations, and undoubtedly many more plied some trade but were too poor to afford a license. "In our village," recalls Tsiporah Rothchild, "all production came from the effort of the craftsmen, with the help of family members. I am reminded of an unusual labor struggle. Aryeh, Reb Nachum

Moishe Pyontkowski's son, decided to strike against his father. And when Reb Nachum Moishe beat the culprit with an iron wheelband, Aryeh yelled with pain and let his father know that 'I am a socialist, I do not want to work overtime at night!'. . . . There were also in Yedwabne 'village tailors,' people who went out to work in other villages."[3]

Itinerant merchants and craftsmen went on their journeys in search of gainful employment for months at a time. There must have been quite a few of them on the road each year. Jewish communities in this area used to call each other by various nicknames. Jews from Radziłów, for example, were called *Radzilower Kozes*—Radziłów goats, an amiable and slightly mocking label; Łomża Jews were nicknamed *Lomzer Baaloonim*, that is, choosy, smug, and somewhat sybaritic in the eyes of their neighbors; Jews from Kolno were known as *Kolner Pekelach-Pekewach*, meaning that they carried loads, or burdens, and were prone to complain a lot; and the Jews from Jedwabne were called *Jedwabne Krichers*, presumably since they were busybodies, moved around so much, and also poked their noses into everything.[4]

As a young man, Rabbi Jacob Baker began his religious education at the famous Yeshiva in Łomża; until his departure from Jedwabne he remained immersed in Talmudic studies (*Yeshiva bokher*) and carried the name of Piekarz, "baker" in Polish. He fondly remembers prewar encounters with Polish neighbors. He lived with his mother, grandmother, and two brothers not far from the Sielawa family compound. Like many other people from the neighborhood, the Piekarz children would occasionally draw water, reputed to be excellent, from the Sielawa well. "One winter nightfall I observed neighbor Sielawa's little girl deliver to Reizele [Jacob Baker's grandmother] a small amount of potato peel for her cow, for which she immediately reimbursed her with a whole gallon of milk. When I wondered at the unequal exchange Reizele explained it thus: 'From the small amount of potato peel we may deduce how little food that family had for supper.' "[5] An elderly Polish pharmacist from Jedwabne, interviewed by Agnieszka Arnold fifty years after the war, also retained a recollection of good neighborly relations between Poles and Jews: "Here there were no such big differences in opinion or whatever, because they were, in this little town, on good terms with the Poles. Depending on each other. Everybody was on a first-name basis, Janek, Icek . . . Life here was, I would say, somehow idyllic."[6]

Contact and interaction among the neighbors were plentiful. And if there was an undercurrent of prudence and caution—Jews were always mindful of a latent hostility nurtured among the surrounding population, especially given that politically the whole area solidly supported the national-democratic party[7]—open confrontation was avoided during the interwar years, and a few situations that could have dangerously escalated were, luckily, defused.

Of course, there were recurrent occasions when Jews were particularly vulnerable to outbursts of antisemitism. In the distant past, when local gentry had periodically convened their territorial assembly and gathered in some locality with a large retinue of servants and acolytes, there had often been brawls, drunkenness, and beatings of local Jews. Easter, when priests evoked in their sermons an image of Jews as God-killers, was a perennial occasion for antisemitic violence. And of course a misfortune could happen at any time because of some unforeseen coincidence. In Jedwabne, for instance, in 1934 a Jewish woman was killed, and a few days later on a market day in a neighboring town a peasant was shot to death. Somehow a rumor began to circulate that the Jedwabne Jews had thus taken revenge on the Poles. Jona Rothchild, the main supplier of iron parts necessary for the reconstruction of the local church, writes in the memorial book that the threat of pogrom (which people anxiously began to anticipate) was averted after Rabbi Białostocki visited the Jedwabne priest, together with Rothchild himself.

This episode fits very well within the boundaries of Jewish existence, which included, among other things, the foreknowledge of impending pogroms (just as during the Second World War ghetto inhabitants almost always knew ahead of time about the coming *Aktion*). Jews took it as a matter of course that in such circumstances secular as well as religious authorities had to be appeased with gifts and enlisted to help avert the coming menace. This was, as it were, an extra tax that the Jews were prepared to pay for protection, and the kehillas (i.e., Jewish communal authorities) had for centuries maintained special funds designated for this purpose.[8]

Until the outbreak of the war Jedwabne was a quiet town, and Jewish lives there differed little from those of their fellows anywhere else in Poland. If anything, they may have been better. The Jewish community was not affected by significant rifts or protracted conflicts. There were a few Chasids in Jedwabne, but spiritual leadership of the community was recognized by all in the person of a pious and respected rabbi, Avigdor Białostocki. A few years before the war the town saw the appointment of a new parish priest, Marian Szumowski, whose sympathies were with the nationalist party, but until then Rabbi Białostocki and Jedwabne's Catholic priest had been on very good terms with each other.[9] In addition, by a lucky coincidence, the local police commander was a decent and straightforward fellow who kept order in the town and went after troublemakers, irrespective of their political beliefs or ethnic background. And then the war came.

SOVIET OCCUPATION, 1939–1941

On August 23, 1939, the German-Soviet Treaty of Non-Aggression was signed in Moscow by Joachim von Ribbentrop and Vyacheslav Molotov—respectively foreign ministers of the Third Reich and the USSR. It has passed into history books under the name "Ribbentrop-Molotov Pact," even though in essence it was an agreement between Hitler and Stalin. The pact opened the way for Hitler to begin the Second World War. He could now launch a military invasion of Poland without the risk of having a "second front" opened against him in the east, by the Soviet Union.

In the secret protocol attached to the pact the two dictators divided the territories that lay between their two countries. "In the event of a territorial and political transformation of the territories belonging to the Polish state," read point 2 of the Secret Additional Protocol, "the spheres of interest of both Germany and the USSR shall be bounded approximately by the line of the rivers Narew, Vistula, and San." As a result over half of the territory of Poland was occupied in September 1939 by the USSR.[1] Hitler's army invaded Poland on September 1, 1939, and the Red Army marched across Poland's eastern border on September 17, 1939. And then the "approximate" demarcation line between the two occupations was finalized in the German-Soviet Boundary and Friendship Treaty signed in Moscow on September 28.

Thus, as we can appreciate from the crowded calendar of these events, initially there was some confusion as to which chunk of Poland belonged to Hitler and which to Stalin. As a result, in the autumn of 1939 Jedwabne was briefly occupied by the Wehrmacht and then surrendered to the Soviet authorities by the Germans, in compliance with the agreed-upon line of demarcation between the two occupations.

Since Jews made up over half of the town's population, undoubtedly some of them took jobs in the town's new administration, or in state-run commerce and manufacturing cooperatives established by the Soviet authorities. But a long memorandum, describing the history of Łomża County under Soviet rule and prepared on the basis of 125 questionnaires filled out by witnesses from the area at the request of the Historical Bureau of the Polish Army in the East (the so-called Anders Army), includes only three general remarks about Jews from Jedwabne, indicating that they displayed zealous support for the Soviet regime.[2] The report covers the entire county, thus encapsulating life experiences of some 170,000 people. Only 16 questionnaires (of the total 125) were filled out by former residents of the *gmina* Jedwabne. Thus, unfortunately, we do not really know any specifics about Jedwabne town life at the time.[3]

But there is no reason to single out Jedwabne as a place where relationships between Jews and the rest of the population during those twenty months of Soviet rule were more antagonistic than anywhere else. In the most detailed study of the town that I located, a former director of the State Archives in Białystok and a historian of the region, Henryk Majecki, provides the names of the five most important officials in the Soviet administration of Jedwabne during this period: "The Chairman of the *raion* [the smallest territorial unit of administration under the Soviet rule] Executive Council in Jedwabne was Danil Kireyevich Sukachov, a well-known activist of the Communist Party of Western Belorussia from before the war"; the first secretary of the *raion* party committee was Mark Timofeevich Rydachenko; members of the secretariat were Piotr Ivanovich Bystrov and Dymitri Borisovich Ustilovski; and, finally, Aleksandr Nikiforovich Malyshev was a secretary of the *Komsomol* (Organization of Communist Youth).[4] Jedwabne was situated in the immediate vicinity of the border, and we can surmise that the local administration was entrusted by the Soviets to experienced personnel brought from the Soviet interior, rather than to local people.

As may be recalled from what I said earlier, residents of the Polish territories taken over by the Soviets in September 1939 often portrayed the Jews as having a privileged relationship with the occupiers. In particular, Polish witnesses evoked their first encounters with the Red Army, which were accompanied, allegedly, by spontaneous outbursts of joy and celebrations by the Jewish population.[5] I found only one statement providing specific information about the kind of reception that the entering Soviet army received from the population of Jedwabne in September 1939. When Agnieszka Arnold interviewed on camera the daughter of Bronisław Śleszyński, in whose barn Jedwabne's Jews were burned in July 1941, she shared the following recollection of this moment:

I saw how the Soviets came in, you know. They went down Przystrzelska Street. Here there was a bakery and a Jew with a Jewess put out a table, it was covered with red cloth, you know, this red cloth was on, and a Polish family. Two Polish families, because these were communists from before the war. . . . And so these three families greeted Soviet soldiers with bread and salt. This I saw. A large banner was attached from one building to another: 'We welcome you' in big letters, they were white, capital letters. And so they greeted with their wives. And then the army at the square, where there is a park now, spread around. I was sixteen years old then, and there were also children. Just children, because older people did not come out to look at this, they were afraid, only from afar, but children have to be everywhere. Well, I was not such a child of prime youth, but we came down there.[6]

Inadvertently, this is a telling description of a rather typical scene—people came out when the Soviets entered town, mostly young people full of curiosity, both Jews and Gentiles. The persistence of the stereotype attributing to Jews a sycophantic attitude toward the Soviets is well reflected in yet another conversation recorded in Jedwabne by Agnieszka Arnold, this time with the elderly local pharmacist, who attempted to explain what collaboration between the Jews and the Soviet administration in Jedwabne entailed: "You know I, I don't know any proofs of this. I only repeat what was, so to speak, a well-known secret. This is what people said. Well, someone had to do it. But I cannot guarantee this with my . . . No, I didn't see anyone do it. I didn't personally know."[7] In other words, this was a stereotype, a cliché, which could be confirmed by anything—by a group of Jewish children cheerfully marching down the street, or by the fact that a Jew worked in the post office (i.e., an official institution), or that some Jewish youth spoke arrogantly to a passerby in the street or to a fellow customer waiting in line in a store. Of course there were "collaborators" or NKVD agents among the Jews, but as we know very well, not exclusively among the Jews—and in Jedwabne, as we shall soon find out, *not even primarily* among the Jews.

But in one respect the *gmina* Jedwabne had a history unlike that of most places under the Soviet occupation. A vast anti-Soviet underground organization had been established there early on, and in June 1940 it was tracked down by the Soviet secret police, NKVD, and destroyed. First, its headquarters in the Kobielno Forest nearby was overwhelmed by an assault of NKVD troops, and a considerable number of people on both sides were killed. And then, since all the documents of the organization were dug out by the Soviets in Kobielno, numerous arrests were made throughout the area. According to a respected Polish historian, Tomasz Strzembosz, knowledgeable about this subject, some 250 people from the vicinity of Jedwabne, Radziłów, and Wizna were imprisoned on this occasion.[8] Many more members of the organization, who feared for their safety, fled from homes and hid in the surrounding forests and swamps. Naturally, a historian investigating the trail of violence in the area would like to know whether any connection can be established between these two extraordinary events: the destruction of the Polish underground organization in June 1940 by the Soviets and the mass murder of the Jews in July 1941 by the Poles.[9]

By sheer coincidence two important testimonies preserved from the period shed interesting light on this story. Corporal Antoni Borawski from the hamlet of Witynie, situated some four kilometers from Jedwabne,[10] left a long narrative curriculum vitae, "My Biography for 1940–1941," with the Historical Bureau of the Anders Army. He had been arrested on July 4th, about two weeks after the shoot-out in the forest, and suffered a long and painful interrogation. But he survived the incarceration and, in the end, was able to tell the tale of betrayal that allowed the Soviet secret police to destroy the underground. Here is how Antoni Borawski told the story in his "biography":

There was one fellow, Dąbrowski from the Ko-łodzieja hamlet, in the headquarters. At the beginning Dąbrowski was a good and exemplary Polish citizen. He supplied armaments to headquarters, traveled a hundred kilometers up to Czerwony Bór, where the Polish army left equipment, and he brought automatic weapons and ammo; when he couldn't get them for free, he would pay what he could. Dąbrowski was a son-in-law of Wiśniewski from Bartki village, and Wiśniewski was a gmina head under the Soviets, and so they agreed with one another as son-in-law with a father-in-law, and Wiśniewski guaranteed that the Soviets would not take him. And Dąbrowski told where the headquarters was and everything, what plans the headquarters had, and that they wanted to attack the Soviets and disarm them. So what happens next? Dąbrowski fled from headquarters, and soon two and two were put together; they realized that something bad would happen and started moving away into the Augustów forests, but still some twenty people remained. *Five machine guns and ammo and a hundred grenades and carbines and the rest were taken to the Augustów forests, and my acquaintance from our hamlet was still at headquarters. They started posting guards along the routes where danger threatened, and keeping a better watch. What next? Dąbrowski contacted his father-in-law, Wiśniewski, and Wiśniewski reported to the NKVD, and the NKVD soon alerted Białystok. Before long the soviets came in forty trucks, they parked trucks ten kilometers away, and they surrounded the forest and swamps and proceeded to tighten the circle and approach headquarters. Only from the direction of Chyliny village was the road open; the sentry had fallen asleep, and when he woke up the sun was rising and the soviets were two hundred meters away, so he ran another three hundred meters and warned our outpost, which opened fire. It was June 22, 1940. The soviets attacked ferociously: they did not take cover but ran straight as boars against the outpost. They suffered big casualties; they said thirty-six were dead and ninety wounded. On our side there were six dead, two wounded, and two women were killed. . . . What happened after the liquidation of the headquarters in Kobielne? I asked the district commander what to do, and he told us, Don't worry, all the books and documents were destroyed, the soviets did not capture anything, there is no danger for us. And so when they liquidated headquarters, for a whole week they stayed in this place looking for weapons and documents. And when the soviets attacked, our people grabbed our documents and buried them under a bush not too far away. The soviets found all our documents, where everybody's last name, first name, and Pseudonym were written down and everything that everybody did. As soon as the soviets found the book, they proceeded to surround entire hamlets where our organization was, and captured all the peasants and looked at the list: those on the list they took to prison, and those who weren't they let go. Mass arrests began, so we didn't wait for them to take us. As soon as night fell, we, all members of the organization, ran away a few kilometers from home, and we were hiding every night for two weeks.*[11]

Borawski managed to stay on the run until July 4th. He identifies in his testimony some half a dozen traitors—one he met face-to-face in prison during a confrontation staged by his captors—and none of them is a Jew. The manager of the cooperative where Borawski was employed, a certain Lewinowicz, was present at the time of Borawski's arrest in Jedwabne. And this is the only Jewish name, and the only reported involvement of a Jew, in the whole affair.[12]

But we have yet another interesting document at our disposal that bears on the matter. Early in 1941, some six months after the Kobielno debacle, the chief of the Białystok District NKVD, Colonel Misiurev, wrote a memo to the secretary of the Białystok District Committee of the CP(b)B (Communist Party of the Bolsheviks of Belorussia), a certain Popov. In this report Misiurev summarized and evaluated activities of the Polish anti-Soviet underground in the Jedwabne region (*raion*) and offered an appraisal of anti-insurgent methods deployed by the NKVD. And he writes in this memo, among other details, that some time after the headquarters in Kobielno was destroyed, an amnesty was proclaimed for all members of the underground organization, on condition that they identify themselves and come out of hiding. By December 25, states Misiurev, 106 people had availed themselves of this opportunity. And then he continues: "From this group we recruited twenty-five people, who are now carrying on further intelligence work."[13] This is an interesting piece of information in its own right. But we should keep it in mind also because it will come back to us in due course from an altogether different source. In any case, the Jews from Jedwabne were not implicated in this whole affair.

T HE OUTBREAK OF THE RUSSO-GERMAN WAR AND THE POGROM IN RADZIŁÓW

What was going on in Jedwabne during the roughly two weeks between the outbreak of the Russo-German war on June 22, 1941, and the massacre of Jews on July 10, we cannot tell exactly. The main source of information on this period remains Wasersztajn's deposition, along with a few remarks dropped by other witnesses. Some people were killed, but the principal threats Jews faced at the time were beatings, confiscation of material property, and humiliations—men caught in the street could be ordered to clean outhouses with their bare hands, for example.[1]

Twenty months of Soviet occupation of this area, from September 1939 to June 1941, took a heavy toll on the local people. They were subjected to the process of sovietization, which affected all nationalities and social classes, but the brunt of propaganda and Soviet repressions was directed against the Polish state. Local elites were arrested or deported. Private property was gradually taken over by the Soviet authorities. A vigorous campaign of secularization targeted all religious institutions and personnel. Consequently, in the summer of 1941 the invading German army was welcomed by the local population of the area (with the exception of Jews, who feared the Nazis more than the Bolsheviks), and Jedwabne was no exception to this rule.[2]

During the trial of Józef Sobuta in 1953, the prosecution tried to establish the circumstances under which Czesław Kupiecki, a local communist, was murdered. Kupiecki worked in the Soviet militia and in the summer of 1941 was immediately identified and denounced to the Germans, as were many other communist sympathizers throughout the area. And even though we cannot tell specifically who was responsible for fingering Kupiecki, it appears that local people were helping the Germans to identify and terrorize their victims from the beginning of the occupation. Thus, on June 22, 1941, Karol Bardoń[3] saw, at the main square in Jedwabne, a group of people covered in blood and standing

with their hands up, first Kupiecki, former volunteer of the Soviet militia, then Wiśniewski, former chairman of the village soviet, third Wiśniewski, secretary of the soviet—these were brothers from the hamlet Bartki in Jedwabne gmina some ten kilometers from Jedwabne [undoubtedly the same people we encountered earlier in Borawski's testimony]—*then three people of Mosaic faith, one of them the owner of the bakery in Jedwabne at the corner of the square and Przestrzelska Street* [probably one of the men who was greeting entering Soviets in September 1939]. *Two others I didn't recognize. These six bleeding individuals were encircled by Germans. In front of the Germans stood a few civilians with thick clubs, to whom a German was calling, Do not kill at once. Slowly, let them suffer. Those civilians doing the beating I didn't recognize, because they were encircled by a group of Germans.*[4]

But the climate of fear among Jedwabne Jews was intensifying by the day, primarily because of rumors about horrible pogroms and killings already carried out in the immediate vicinity. A Jew from Radziłów, Menachem Finkelsztajn, reports that on July 7, 1941, some 1,500 Jews were killed in his native village. Two days earlier, on July 5th, in nearby Wąsosz, 1,200 had been murdered. About Jedwabne Finkelsztajn writes that during a pogrom lasting three days, some 3,300 Jews were killed there. The perpetrators of these horrors, which took place with the Germans' consent, were "local hooligans," as he put it. Finkelsztajn may have his numbers inflated roughly by a factor of two: in a lengthy testimony that I quote below, written in longhand and deposited alongside his other testimony at the Jewish Historical Institute, he gives 800 as the number of Jewish victims in Radziłów, not 1,500, and his figure for Jedwabne victims above is also too high. But his numbers do properly reflect the scale of these dramatic events—that is, many hundreds, rather than a dozen or so, were killed.[5]

Deafening noise of artillery barrage woke up inhabitants of the Radziłów village in Grajewo County on June 22, 1941. Huge clouds of dust and smoke on the horizon, from the direction of the German border, which was but twenty kilometers away, indicated that something important was afoot. The news about the outbreak of war between the Soviet Union and Hitler-Germany spread like wildfire. The eight hundred Jewish inhabitants of the village immediately understood the seriousness of the situation. The proximity of a bloodthirsty enemy filled everyone with fear. . . .

On the 23rd a few Jews managed to escape from the village to Białystok. All the other Jewish inhabitants left town, setting off for fields and nearby hamlets to avoid the first encounter with the bloodthirsty enemy, whose murderous designs against the Jews were very well known. The attitude of peasants toward the Jews was very bad. They didn't allow the Jews even to enter their farmsteads. The same day when the Germans arrived, peasants chased away the Jews, cursing and threatening them. Jews had no other choice but to return to their homes. Poles from the vicinity ridiculed frightened Jews and, motioning across their necks, kept saying, "Now it will be cut up Jude" [Teraz będzie rżnij Jude]. The Polish population immediately cozied up to the Germans. They built a triumphal arch to greet the German army decorated with a swastika, a portrait of Hitler, and a sign: "Long live the German army, which *liberated us from the horrible grip of the Judeo-commune!" The first question hooligans asked was: Is it permitted to kill the Jews? Of course the Germans gave a positive answer. And immediately afterward they started to persecute the Jews. They started telling various false things about Jews and set Germans against them. Those Germans beat Jews mercilessly and robbed them of their property and then distributed stolen items among the Poles. Then they proposed a watch phrase, "Don't sell anything to eat to the Jews." And so the Jewish situation got even worse. Germans, in order to put down the Jews, took their cows away and gave them to the Poles. It also became known that Polish bandits killed a Jewish girl, sawed off her head, and threw the body in the swamp, feet first. . . .*

On the 24th Germans ordered all males to assemble near the synagogue. Immediately people understood what that meant. They started running away from the town, but Poles kept a watch over all the roads and brought back those who ran away. Only a few managed to escape, including myself and my father. In the meantime German soldiers proceeded to give lessons of "good manners" toward the Jews. These "lessons" took place in the presence of many assembled Poles.

Soldiers ordered the Jews to bring out all the holy books and Torahs from the synagogue and the prayer house and burn them. When the Jews refused, Germans ordered them to unroll the Torahs and to douse them with kerosene, and they set them alight. They ordered Jews to sing and dance around the huge burning pile. Around the dancing Jews a jeering crowd was assembled that beat them freely. When the holy books burned down, they harnessed Jews to carts and ordered them to pull while beating mercilessly. Jews had to pull them all over town. Screams of pain were frequently piercing the air. But together with these screams one could hear happily screaming Polish and German sadists who were sitting in the carts. Poles and Germans continued to torment the Jews until they chased them to a swampy little river near the town. Jews were ordered there to undress completely and to get up to their necks in the swamp. Sick and old men, who could not obey these beastly orders, were beaten up and thrown into even deeper swamps.

. . . From this day on a horrible chain of sufferings and torments began for the Jews. Poles were the main tormentors, as they mercilessly beat men, women, and children, irrespective of their age. They also sent Germans at every opportunity, by insinuating things. And so on the 26th of June, on Friday evening, they sent a group of German soldiers to our house. Like wild animals the tormentors dispersed around the house searching and throwing around everything they found. Anything of value they took and put on carts waiting in front of the house. They were bursting with joy. They stomped in their heavy boots over household items, which they had thrown to the ground; foodstuffs they also threw out and doused with kerosene.

Germans were accompanied by Poles, whose leader, Henryk Dziekoński, later would also distinguish himself by barbarity. He destroyed everything with an even greater ferocity. He broke tables, wardrobes, and candelabras. When they finished destroying things, they started beating my father. Escape was impossible because the house was surrounded by soldiers. . . .

Much more painful than wounds and damages we suffered this evening was the awareness that our situation was much worse on account of the Polish population taking a hostile attitude toward the Jews. And they were becoming more active and bold in their persecutions.

Next morning a group of prominent town citizens came to our house, together with our acquaintance *Wolf Szlepen*[?], *who was a well-known Zionist activist and speaker, and everybody tried in vain to comfort us. No solution was found. The political news was overwhelming. . . . Even though we were all persuaded that the Germans would be defeated, one could see that the war would last a long time. Who would be able to survive this? Jews were like a defenseless lamb in the midst of a pack of wolves. One could feel, it was in the air, that the Polish population was getting ready for a pogrom. That's why we all decided that my mother should go and plead with the local priest, Aleksander Dolegowski, whom we knew well. We wanted him, as a spiritual leader of the community, to influence the believers not to take part in persecution of the Jews. But how great was our disappointment when the priest, with anger, replied, "It is well known that every Jew, from the youngest to those sixty years old, are communists," and said that he had no interest whatsoever in defending them. My mother tried to argue that his position was false, that even if someone deserved to be punished, women and small children were surely innocent? She appealed to his conscience to have pity and stop a dark mob that was ready to commit all kinds of atrocities that in the future would certainly stand as a* shame to the Polish nation, because the political situation would not always remain as it was then. But his cruel heart did not soften, and he said in the end that he could not say anything good about the Jews, because his believers would throw mud on him. The same answer was received from all the other prominent Christian town citizens to whom Jews appealed to intervene in this matter.

The consequences of these refusals were not long in coming. On the very next day squads of young Polish sons were organized: the Kosmaczewski brothers, Józef Anton, and Leon, Feliks Mordaszewicz, Kosak, Ludwik Weszczewski [?], and others who inflicted terrible moral and physical pain on frightened and miserable Jews. From morning till night they led old Jews, laden with sacred books, to a nearby river. They were sent on their march by crowds of Christian women, children, and men. When they got to the river, the Jews had to throw their books into the water. They also had to lie down, get up, hide their heads, swim, and perform other idiotic exercises. Spectators laughed loudly and applauded. Murderers stood over their victims and beat them mercilessly if they didn't execute an order. They also took women and girls and ordered them to get wet in the river.

On the way back squads armed with sticks and iron bars surrounded the tired, barely alive Jews and gave them a beating. And when one of the tortured protested, refused to obey orders, and threatened and cursed them, saying that they would be taken to account for this soon, they beat him so that he lost consciousness. After nightfall squads assaulted Jews in their houses, by breaking down windows and doors. They took the hated Jews out, beat them till the Jews fell down bloodied and unconscious. Not even women and children, or mothers with newborn babies, were spared. From time to time they brought Jews from their houses to the square and they beat them there. The screams were unbearable. Around the tortured ones crowds of Polish men, women, and children were standing and laughing at the miserable victims who were falling under the blows of the bandits. There were many wounded and mortally sick Jews as a result of these orgies. And their number was increasing day by day. The only Polish doctor who was in town, Jan Mazurek, refused medical assistance to people who had been beaten.

The situation was worsening day by day. The Jewish population became a toy in the hands of the Poles. There were no German authorities as *the army moved on and did not leave power to anyone.*

The only one who had influence and maintained some sort of order was the priest, who mediated between Christians in their affairs. It was not simply that the Jews were of no concern to anybody; propaganda started coming out from the upper echelons of Polish society which influenced the mob, stating that it was time to settle scores with those who had crucified Jesus Christ, with those who take Christian blood for matzoh and are a source of all evil in the world—the Jews. Let's stop playing around with the Jews. It is time to cleanse Poland of these pests and bloodsuckers. The seed of hatred fell on well-nourished soil, which had been prepared for many years by the clergy.

The wild and bloodthirsty mob took it as a holy challenge that history had put upon it—to get rid of the Jews. And the desire to take over Jewish riches whetted their appetites even more.

The Poles were in charge, since not even a single German was present. On Sunday July 6th, at midday a lot of Poles from the neighboring town of Wąsosz came to Radziłów. It was immediately known that those who came had previously killed in a horrible manner, using pipes [?] and knives, all the Jews in their own town, not sparing even women or little children. A horrible panic broke out. People understood that this was a tragic signal of destruction. Immediately all the Jews, from little children to old men, fled the town for neighboring fields and forests. No Christian let any Jew into his house or offered any help. Our family also ran into the fields, and when it got dark, we hid in a field of wheat. Late at night we heard subdued calls for help not far from us. We covered up our presence as best we could, understanding that over there the fate of a Jewish life was being decided. Calls were getting fainter, and then they subsided. We didn't speak one word to each other then, even though we felt that we had so much to say, but it was better to be silent since there was nothing that could be said to lift our spirits. We were sure that some Jews had been murdered. Who killed them? Polish murderers, dirty hands of people from the underworld, people who were blinded and driven by animal instinct to kill and rob, who had been raised for decades by a reactionary clergy, who bolstered their existence by preaching racial hatred. Why? What wrong had we done? This was the most painful question that multiplied our suffering, but there was no one to complain to. Whom to tell about our inno-

cence and the great injustice that history had thrown our way? In the morning Poles spread the news that the murderers from Wąsosz were chased away, and that Jews could safely return home. Exhausted and tired everybody started to walk across the fields toward town thinking that the news was truthful, but they shuddered at a horrible sight that they encountered upon coming closer.

In the vicinity of the town the two dead bodies of Moses Reznel [?] and his daughter (whom we had heard as they were being murdered) were brought. They were then taken to the square where later the execution of all the Jews would be carried out. As if to witness some horrible miracle all the Poles, from children to elders, men and women, were running, with joy on their faces, to see the victims who had been clubbed to death by Polish murderers. Before burial the girl opened her eyes and sat up—clearly she had just lost consciousness from the beating—but the murderers did not pay attention and buried her alive together with her father.

To the newly established Polish municipal authorities made up of the priest, the doctor, a former secretary of the gmina Stanisław Grzymkowski, and a few other prominent Poles a delegation was sent to plead with them to stop what the popu-

lation was doing. They replied that they could not help and sent the Jews to people from the underworld, to negotiate with them. Those in turn said that the Jews should compensate them, and then everybody's lives would be spared. Jews, thinking that this might be their last chance, started bringing to Wolf Szlepen [?] various valuables: china, suits, sewing machines [?], gifts of silver and gold; they also promised to give up last cows that they had hidden. But all this was a comedy organized by murderers. The fate of Radziłów's Jews was already sealed. As was later learned, the Polish population knew one day ahead when the Jews would be liquidated and in what manner. But no one . . .

And after these words half of a large sheet of paper on which Finkelsztajn penciled concluding parts of his recollection about the mass murder of Radziłów Jews is missing. The next sheet, the very last one, has been preserved intact. He brings the matter to a close in the following manner:

What a terrible sight this presented can be gauged from the fact that the Germans stated that the Poles had gone overboard. The arrival of

*the Germans saved eighteen Jews who had man-
aged to hide during the pogrom. There was an
eight-year-old boy among them, who had already
been buried, but who revived and dug himself
out. . . . In this manner the Jewish community in
Radziłów was wiped off the face of the earth after
five hundred years of existence. Together with the
Jews everything Jewish was destroyed in the village as well: the study house, the synagogue, and
the cemetery.*[6]

Finkelsztajn's narrative found an unexpected
confirmation sixty years later. In July of 2000,
an elderly inhabitant of Radziłów who wished
to remain anonymous spoke about the pogrom: "Neither on this day [when the pogrom
took place] nor on the preceeding day did I
see any Germans coming from the outside to
Radziłów. A gendarme stood on the balcony
and looked at the scene. But our people did it.
In fact on the previous day, on Sunday, July
6, a lot of people came to Radziłów by horse-
drawn carts from Wąsosz, where a pogrom
had taken place a day earlier." Stanisław Ramotowski, another elderly Pole from the vicinity of Radziłów, interviewed on the same
occasion, confirms that people knew one day

in advance about the pending pogrom. He was told about it by a certain Malinowski from Czerwonki, and thus could forewarn and save some Jewish friends, including a woman whom he later married.[7]

As a result of those pogroms many Jews from surrounding villages, including one of my interlocutors, Wiktor NiełAwicki, sought shelter in Jedwabne during those days. Nieławicki was from Wizna, where the Germans, immediately upon entering, carried out executions of scores of Jewish males. But since Wizna Jews were not Chasidic and looked very much like their Polish neighbors, German executioners needed help from local Polish informants to identify their victims. In this manner some seventy Jewish males were picked up from a few houses still standing after German bombardment—near the town square, where the Jews had assembled—and taken to be shot in a nearby ditch. From a smith's house at Srebrowska Street, where several Jewish families had taken shelter, another dozen were killed on the spot. Jews were frantically running around to find a safer place, and many ended up in Jedwabne.

Among them Niełąwicki fled there with his parents to seek temporary shelter at the house of his uncle, Pecynowicz. "In Yedwabne it was still quiet," he writes in the Jedwabne memorial book. Leaders of the Jewish community delivered silver candlesticks to the Catholic bishop of Łomża and sought assurance that he would not permit a pogrom in Jedwabne and would intervene with the Germans on behalf of the Jewish community. "Yes, the Bishop kept his word for a while. But the Jews placed too much confidence in his promise and refused to listen to the constant warnings that came from friendly Gentile neighbors. My Uncle and his rich brother Eliyahu did not believe me when I told them what had happened in Wizno. 'And if it had happened there,' they said, 'we here in Yedwabne are safe because the Bishop promised to protect us.' "[8]

PREPARATIONS

In the meantime Jedwabne's municipal authorities were constituting themselves. Marian Karolak became the mayor, and among his closest collaborators we can identify a certain Wasilewski and Józef Sobuta.[1] What municipal authorities were doing during those days, again, we cannot tell precisely, beyond recognizing that they consulted with the Germans and eventually carried out the mass murder of Jedwabne Jews.

Local people knew what was coming ahead of time (just as they had known in Radziłów). Both Dvojra Pecynowicz, Nieławicki's cousin, and Mietek Olszewicz (one of the seven Jews mentioned in Wasersztajn's testimony, who were later hidden by the Wyrzykowski family) were warned by their Polish friends about the impending catastrophe. When the sixteen-year-old Nieławicki urged his uncles to take note of these warnings and hide for the day, they dismissed him, pointing out that Jews had lived in Warsaw under the German occupation for two years already, and scoffed that he was talking nonsense. But many local people must have shared advance knowledge of the impending pogrom, or else peasants from neighboring hamlets would not have converged on Jedwabne starting at dawn on July 10th, as if it were a market day (which it was not).[2]

The massacre of Jedwabne Jews on July 10, 1941, was coordinated by the town's mayor, Marian Karolak. His name appears in virtually every deposition. He issued orders to others and was himself otherwise, more practically, engaged throughout the pogrom. He is certainly the evil spirit of this tragedy. A few other people identified in leading roles that day were also employed in the town council. A road watchman, Mieczysław Gerwad, put it simply: "The entire town council participated in this murder of Jews."[3]

Where the initiative came from—whether it originated with the Germans (as per Wasersztajn's phrase, "such an order was issued by the Germans"), or with the town council members of Jedwabne—is impossible to settle once and for all. But it is also an academic question, since both sides apparently quickly agreed on the matter, and on the method of its implementation. "At the instruction of my brother Zygmunt Laudański I went to work for the gendarmerie in Jedwabne," states Jerzy Laudański, one of the youngest, barely nineteen years old at the time, and among the most brutal participants in these events,

and in 1941 four or five gestapo men came in a taxi and started talking in the city hall; what they talked about I don't know. After a certain time Karolak Marian told us Poles to call Polish citizens to the town hall. After calling in the Polish population, he ordered them to round up the Jews to the square, presumably to work, and this was done. At that time I also participated in herding the Jews onto the square."[4]

The visit of the Gestapo men to Jedwabne is confirmed by many sources. But they do not agree on details—did it take place on the day of the pogrom, for example, or the day before? "Before the start of this mass murder," writes Karol Bardoń, "I saw in front of the Jedwabne town hall a few gestapo men, but I don't remember if it was on the day of the mass murder or the day before."[5] That the town council signed some "agreement with the gestapo" about the burning of the Jews we are also told by Henryk Krystowczyk, but he did not witness the events and only repeats what he has heard "from various people."[6] But we cannot expect to learn about the agreement from any eyewitness or participant, since the only town council member who left a deposition is Józef Sobuta, and his testimony is less than forthcoming. It is clear, in any case, that the town council and the Germans agreed to the murder of the Jedwabne Jews.

What specifics had been agreed upon are a secondary matter. Murderous intent toward their neighbors was manifested by the Polish population in Jedwabne not just verbally, when the town council members spoke with the Germans, but through actual deeds carried out by the town population. In all likelihood the municipal authorities were given a certain amount of time—eight hours, if we are to take literally an angry reprimand by the gendarmerie commander, which I quote below—to do with the Jews as they pleased.[7] What we would like to know, however, with as much precision as possible, is this: What specific role did the Germans play in the implementation of the massacre? How many of them were in town on that day, and what did they do?

There was an outpost of German gendarmerie in Jedwabne, staffed by eleven men.[8] We can also infer from various sources that a group of Gestapo men arrived in town by taxi either on that day or the previous one. According to Józef Żyluk, "it was like this: I was cutting hay, and the mayor of Jedwabne, Karolak, came to me in the meadow and said to go and bring all the Jews into the square. And so we both went."[9]

In the sources at our disposal the term "gendarmes" (or, actually, far more frequently "a gendarme") appears as part of an explanation describing the circumstances that led several of the accused in the Ramotowski trial to appear in the market square or near the barn. Thus, in a rather typical deposition, Czesław Lipiński tells the court how Jurek Laudański,

Eugeniusz Kalinowski, "and one German" came to fetch him, and how he went with them to round up Jews to the square;[10] Feliks Tarnacki was visited by Karolak and Wasilewski, who "together with a gestapo man chased [me] to the square" and told him to guard the Jews.[11] Miciura, who was employed this day at the gendarmerie outpost doing some carpentry work, was told by a gendarme at some point "to go to the square to watch the Jews." And his is the only case in which a lone gendarme orders anyone into action. Otherwise, the gendarme always appears making rounds in the company of some members of the town council.[12]

Now, let us understand the broader context in which the murders took place. At the time the overall undisputed bosses over life and death in Jedwabne were the Germans. No sustained organized activity could take place there without their consent.[13] They were the only ones who could decide the fate of the Jews. It was within their power also to stop the murderous pogrom at any time. And they did not choose to intervene. If they suggested that some Jewish families be spared, they must have done so without serious conviction, for all the Jews on whom the murderers lay their hands were killed in the end. And, ironically, on that day the outpost of the German gendarmerie was the safest place in town for the Jews, and a few survived only because they happened to be there at the time. But it is also clear that had Jedwabne not been occupied by the Germans, the Jews of Jedwabne would not have been murdered by their neighbors. This is not a gratuitous observation—the tragedy of Jedwabne Jewry is but an episode in the murderous war that Hitler waged against all Jews. As to the Germans' direct participation in the mass murder of Jews in Jedwabne on July 10, 1941, however, one must admit that it was limited, pretty much, to their taking pictures.

W HO MURDERED THE JEWS OF JEDWABNE?

Edward Śleszyński: "In the barn of my father, Bronisław Śleszyński, a lot of Jews were burned. I didn't see it with my own eyes since I was in the bakery on that day, but I know from people who lived in Jedwabne at the time that Poles carried out this deed. Germans participated only in photographing."[1] Bolesław Ramotowski: "I want to stress that Germans did not participate in the murder of Jews; they just stood and took pictures of how Poles mistreated the Jews."[2] Mieczysław Gerwad: "Jews were being murdered by the Polish population."[3]

Julia Sokołowska worked at the time as a cook for the gendarmes. When she was questioned during the investigation of the case against Ramotowski, on January 11, 1949, she made the following deposition:

A few days after the German occupying army entered Polish territory in 1941, inhabitants of Jedwabne, together with the Germans, started to kill Jews living in the town of Jedwabne, where they killed over one and a half thousand people of Jewish nationality. I stress that I did not see any Germans beating the Jews. The Germans even brought three Jewish women to the gendarmerie outpost and said to make sure that they didn't get killed, so I locked them up and gave the key to the gendarme who had told me to lock them up, and he ordered me to give them something to eat, so I prepared something and I brought it to them. When everything was over and things calmed down, these Jewish women were let go, and they lived in a house near the gendarmerie and came to work at the gendarmerie outpost. Germans did not beat the Jews; the Polish population bestially massacred the Jews, and Germans only stood to the side and took pictures, and later they showed how Poles killed the Jews.[4]

Sokołowska then proceeds to enumerate fifteen names of individuals or entire families (fathers with sons, for instance, or brothers) who took an active part in the massacre. She points out who beat the Jews with a wooden club, and who used a "rubber [truncheon]," and adds one more interesting detail about German input into the events of this day: "I was a cook in the gendarmerie at the time, and I saw how Eugeniusz Kalinowski approached the commander of the gendarmes asking that he issue him weapons because "they" didn't want to go—he didn't say who didn't want to go. The commander jumped to his feet and said, I will not give you weapons; do what you want. Then Kalinowski turned around and quickly ran outside the town where they were chasing these Jews."[5]

In the context of her detailed and incriminating deposition it is very interesting to note a shift in the witness's demeanor four months later, when the trial against Ramotowski and accomplices was held in May. The accused, as mentioned earlier, did not speak much during the trial, and they informed the court that they had been beaten during interrogation. Sokołowska was also reluctant to speak on the witness stand, and then she uttered this extraordinary sentence: "On the critical day there were sixty gestapo men, because I cooked dinner for them, and there were a lot of gendarmes because they came from other outposts."[6] For the first time we learn that there were a substantial number of Germans in Jedwabne on the day of the murder, and the person who reveals this information cooked a meal for them and therefore should know.

I cannot account satisfactorily for this change in the demeanor of the accused and Sokołowska as well. After all, they were just as much at the mercy of the security police sitting in a courtroom in Łomża in May 1949 as they had been four months earlier in investigative detention. On the other hand, as we know, this was not a high priority trial for the authorities. And the accused had families and friends in the vicinity who knew each other, and could easily realize (they also shared defense attorneys) that they had for the most part incriminated themselves and each other. Finally, they also had plenty of time to activate on their own behalf assorted instruments of informal pressure potent in a small-town community.

In the closing years of the German occupation a very strong Polish nationalist underground organization—National Armed Forces (NSZ)—was active in this area, and many people "stayed in the forest" after the war. A brutal, quasi–civil war went on in the Białystok voivodeship for years after the "people's Poland" had been established. Jedwabne, for instance, was taken over for a few hours as late as September 29, 1948, by an armed detachment of a certain "Wiarus" ("Old Veteran").[7] Not only the communist secret police but also "boys from the forest" were feared by people in this area long after the war officially ended. One can easily imagine how an elderly old maid, and thus presumably a person of low standing in a small-town community, could be persuaded to modify testimony that otherwise implicated a large number of the town's citizens.[8] And besides, as we have already seen, the Security Office was not terribly keen to prosecute this case vigorously.

But irrespective of whether there was any pressure on Sokołowska, her court testimony did not remain unchallenged. On August 9, 1949, from his prison cell in Warsaw, Karol Bardoń—the only accused in this trial who was condemned to death—sent a "supplement" to his earlier appeal of the verdict to the Łomża District Court:

During court proceedings witness Sokołowska Julia, a former cook at the gendarmerie outpost in Jedwabne, stated that on the day of the mass murder of Jews allegedly sixty gestapo men and the same number of gendarmes were around, and that she cooked dinner for the gestapo men. This statement is untrue, because on that day I was working in the courtyard of the gendarmerie outpost and I did not see any gestapo men or gendarmes. Going a few times to a toolshed that was on the estate [of a local nobleman], *I walked across the square where Jews were assembled, and I did not see any gestapo men or gendarmes there either. Likewise, it is absurd to claim that one cooked on a small stove a dinner for sixty people.*

After the killing of Jews was carried out, a few civilians ran into the courtyard of the gendarmerie outpost where I was repairing a car and tried to grab three Jews who were chopping wood. Then the commander of the outpost, Adamy, came out and said, Was eight hours not enough for you to do with the Jews as you please? From the above it is clear that the mass murder of the

Jews was not carried out by the Gestapo, whom I did not see that day, but by the local population under the leadership of mayor Karolak.[9]

Bardoń revisited this episode three years later in a very interesting autobiography that he sent to the president of the Polish People's Republic as an attachment to his appeal for clemency. And this time he approached the subject, so to speak, from the other end of the gastrointestinal tract: "In the courtyard out-houses were standing, and if there were sixty gestapo men and sixty gendarmes who came for this action of mass murder, some of them would have to be in the courtyard as well." And then he finished his autobiography with the following sentence: "During this day of mass murder I walked three times to the tool-shed, some 350–400 meters away, and in the streets to dinner and back, and I did not see a single uniformed individual either in the streets or by the group of people assembled in the square."[10] I do not think that a convict pleading for mercy would write such things in support of his clemency appeal just to endear himself to the president of Poland. Surely the latter could be presumed to more eagerly welcome news confirming that the Germans, rather than his fellow citizens, had murdered the Jews.

Sources at our disposal cite, by my count, ninety-two names (and, often, home addresses to boot) of people who participated in the murders of Jedwabne Jews. Perhaps not all of them should be labeled murderers—after all, nine of the accused in the Łomża trials were found not guilty.[11] Various people who guarded the Jews in the square may perhaps have just been there, uninvolved in acts of brutality.[12] On the other hand we also know that people mentioned by name are only a fraction of those who were there at the time. "Near the assembled Jews," states Władysław Miciura, another defendant in Ramotowski's trial, "there was a mass of people not only from Jedwabne but also from the environs."[13] "A lot of people were there, whose names I do not remember now," we are told by Zygmunt Laudański who with his brother was among the busiest on this day, "I'll tell them as soon as I recall."[14] The crowd of perpetrators swelled somehow as Jews were being herded toward the barn where they were incinerated. As Bolesław Ramotowski put it, "when we were chasing them to the barn, I couldn't see, because it was very crowded."[15]

The accused, who all resided in Jedwabne during the war, could not identify many participants, because a large number of these were peasants who flocked into town from neighboring hamlets. "There were many peasants from hamlets whom I didn't know," explains Miciura. "These were for the most part young men who enjoyed this catching of the Jews, and they tortured them."[16]

In other words, a lot of people took an active part in this massacre. It was a mass murder in a double sense—on account of both the number of victims and the number of perpetrators. Again, ninety-two participants were singled out by name. These were all adult men, residents of the town of Jedwabne. What does this number signify?

Before the war, we recall, some 2,500 people lived in the town, with Jews making up about two-thirds of this total. If we divide the ethnically Polish population in half, we get about 450 male Polish residents, including children and elderly. Let us divide this number in half again, and we will have to conclude that roughly 50 percent of the adult men of Jed-

wabne are identified by name among participants in the pogrom.

How was the killing carried out? According to folklore preserved in Jedwabne to
this day, it was a very cruel affair. The Jedwabne pharmacist whose interview with the
filmmaker Agnieszka Arnold I quoted earlier
repeats almost verbatim the words we have already heard from the lips of another witness:
"A certain gentleman told me about this, Mr.
Kozłowski, who is no longer alive. He was a
butcher. Very decent man. His son-in-law was
a prosecutor before the war. From a very good
family. And he told me that one could not look
at what was going on."[17] Yet another elderly
Polish woman, Halina Popiołek, who was a
young girl at the time and now careful to preface her interview with a journalist of *Gazeta
Pomorska* with the assertion that she "did not
see everything," spoke in more detail: "I was
not present when they were beheading Jews,
or piercing them to death with sharp spikes. I
also did not see how our people ordered young
Jewesses to drown in a pond. My mother's sister saw it. She was all in tears when she came
to tell us about this. I saw how they ordered
young Jewish boys to take off Lenin's monu-

ment, how they were told to carry it around and shout, 'War is because of us.' I saw how they were beaten at the time with rubber truncheons, how Jews were massacred in the synagogue, and how the massacred Lewiniuk, who was still breathing, was buried alive by our people. . . . They chased them all to a barn. Poured kerosene all around. It took but two minutes, but the scream . . . I can still hear it.[18]

So it was not only the the sight of the massacre of Jews that was unbearable. Also, the screams of tormented people were numbing, as was the smell of their burning bodies. The slaughter of Jedwabne Jews lasted an entire day, and it was confined to a space no bigger than a sports stadium. Śleszyński's barn, where the majority of the pogrom victims were burned in the afternoon, was but a stone's throw from the square in the center of town. The Jewish cemetery, where many of the victims were knifed, clubbed, and stoned to death, is just across the road. And so everybody who was in town on this day and in possession of a sense of sight, smell, or hearing either participated in or witnessed the tormented deaths of the Jews of Jedwabne.

T HE MURDER

It all begun, as we remember, with the convocation on the morning of July 10th of all adult Polish males to Jedwabne's town hall. But rumors about the planned assault on the Jews must have been circulating earlier. Otherwise, carts full of people from nearby hamlets would not have been converging on the town on this day since early dawn. I suspect that some of these people were veterans of murderous pogroms that had recently been carried out in the vicinity. It was typical, when a "wave of pogroms" swept over some area, that in addition to local participants unique to each locality, a core group of plunderers kept moving from place to place.[1]

"On a certain day, at the request of Karolak and Sobuta, several dozen men assembled in front of the city hall in Jedwabne and were equipped by the German gendarmerie and Karolak and Sobuta with whips and clubs. Then Karolak and Sobuta ordered the assembled men to bring to the square in front of the town hall all the Jews of Jedwabne." In an earlier testimony witness Danowski added one more detail to this crisp narrative by pointing out that people were served vodka on the occasion, though nobody else confirmed this.[2]

More or less at the same time that Poles were called to the town hall, Jews were ordered to assemble at the square for, allegedly, some cleaning duty. Rivka Fogel recalled that she meant to bring along a broom. Since Jews had previously been pressed into debasing cleanup jobs, one could imagine at first that this was to be but a routine exercise in humiliation. "My husband took our two children and went there. I stayed at home for a while trying to put things in order and lock the doors and windows properly."[3] But it became clear almost instantly that the circumstances were somehow different on that day. Mrs. Fogel did not follow her husband and children to the square; instead, together with a neighbor, Mrs. Pravde, she hid in the nearby garden of a noblemen's estate. And a few moments later "we could hear from there the terrible cries of a young boy, Joseph Levin, whom the goyim were beating to death."[4]

By some uncanny coincidence we learn from the testimony of Karol Bardoń, who happened to be passing by in the vicinity a few moments later, that Lewin had been stoned to death. Bardoń, we recall, was repairing a car this morning in the courtyard of the German gendarmerie's outpost and had to go to the toolshed on the nobleman's estate (in whose garden the two women were hiding). "Around the corner from the foundry adjacent to the toolshed an inhabitant of Jedwabne, Wiśniewski, was standing. . . . Wiśniewski called me, and I came closer and Wiśniewski pointed to a massacred cadaver of a young man of Mosaic persuasion, about twenty-two years old, whose name was Lewin, and said to me, Look, mister, we killed this SOB with stones. . . . Wiśniewski showed me a stone weighing twelve to fourteen kilograms and said, I smacked him good with this stone and he won't get up any more."[5] This took place at the very beginning of the pogrom. As Bardoń writes, on his way to the toolshed he saw a group of only about a hundred Jews on the square; by the time he was on his way back, the assemblage had grown considerably.

In another part of town Wincenty Goś-cicki had just returned home from a night watchman's job. "In the morning when I went to bed, my wife came and told me to get up and said that bad things were going on. Near our house people were beating Jews with clubs. I got up then and went outside the house. Then I was called by Urbanowski who told me, Look what is going on, and showed me four Jewish corpses. These were 1. Fiszman, 2. the two Styjakowskis [?] and Blubert. I, then, I hid in the house."[6]

From early on that day the Jews understood that they were in mortal danger. Many tried to escape into neighboring fields, but only a few succeeded. It was difficult to get out of town without being noticed, as small vigilante groups of peasants were milling around trying to ferret out and catch hiding and fleeing Jews. A dozen teenagers grabbed

Nieławicki, who was already in the fields when the pogrom began, as he was trying to sneak across the fields to Wizna. He was beaten up and brought to the square. Similarly Olszewicz was caught in the fields by peasant youths, beaten up, and brought back to town. Some one to two hundred people managed to run away, hide, and survive that day—among them, as we know, Nieławicki and Olszewicz. But many others were killed on the spot, right where they were apprehended. On his trip to the toolshed Bardoń saw "on the left side of the road, in the fields belonging to the estate, *civilians* [author's emphasis] mounted on horses, wielding thick wooden clubs," who were patrolling the area.[7] A horseman could easily spot people hiding in the fields and then catch up with them. Jedwabne Jews were doomed.

On this day a cacophony of violence swept through the town. It unfolded in the form of many uncoordinated, simultaneous initiatives over which Karolak and the town council exercised only general supervision (as we remember, they went around enlisting people for guard duty on the square, for example). They monitored progress and made sure at critical junctures that the goal of the pogrom was advanced. But otherwise people were free to improvise as best they knew how.

Bardoń, on his way to the toolshed one more time later in the day, he stumbled on Wiśniewski in the same place as before, near Lewin's body.

I understood that Wiśniewski was waiting here for something. I took all the necessary parts from the toolshed, and on my way back I met the same two young men whom I had seen when I went to the toolshed for the first time that morning [he later identifies them as Jerzy Laudański and Kalinowski]. *I understood that they were coming to Wiśniewski to the place where Lewin had been killed, and they were bringing another man of Mosaic persuasion, a married owner of the mechanical mill where I had been employed till March 1939, called Hersh Zdrojewicz. They held him under the arms and blood was flowing from his head over his neck and onto his torso. Zdrojewicz said to me, Save me, Mister Bardoń. Being afraid of these murderers, I replied, I cannot help you with anything, and I passed them by.*[8]

And thus in one part of town Laudański with Wiśniewski and Kalinowski were stoning to death Lewin and Zdrojewicz; in front of Gościcki's house four Jews were clubbed to death by somebody else; in the pond near Łomżyńska Street a certain "Łuba Władysław . . . drowned two Jewish blacksmiths";[9] in still another location Czesław Mierzejewski raped and then killed Judes Ibram;[10] the beautiful Gitele Nadolny (Nadolnik), the youngest daughter of the *melamed* (kheyder teacher), whom everybody knew because they had learned to read in her father's house, had her head cut off, and the murderers, we are told, later kicked it around;[11] at the square "Dobrzańska asked for water [it was a hot summer day], then fainted; no one was allowed to help her, and her mother was killed because she wanted to bring water; [while] Betka Brzozowska was killed with a baby in her arms."[12] Jews were mercilessly beaten all this time, and their houses, in the meantime, were plundered.[13]

Simultaneously with multiple individual actions, more organized forms of persecution were also engulfing Jewish victims, who were driven in groups to the cemetery to be killed wholesale. "They took healthier men and chased them to the cemetery and ordered them to dig a pit, and after it was dug out, Jews were killed every which way, one with iron, another with a knife, still another with a club."[14] "Stanisław Szelawa was murdering with an iron hook, [stabbing] in the stomach. The witness [Szmul Wasersztajn, whose second deposition held in the Jewish Historical Institute I am now quoting] was hiding in the bushes. He heard the screaming. They killed twenty-eight men in one place from among the strongest. Szelawa took away one Jew. His tongue was cut off. Then a long silence."[15] The murderers got excited and were working at a frantic pace. "I stood on Przytulska Street," said an older woman, Bronisława Kalinowska, "and Jerzy Laudański, inhabitant of Jedwabne, was running down the street, and he said that he had already killed two or three Jews; he was very nervous and ran along."[16]

But it must soon have become apparent that fifteen hundred people cannot be killed by such primitive methods in a day. So the perpetrators decided to kill all the Jews at once, by burning them together. This very same method had been used a few days earlier, during the Radziłów pogrom. For whatever reason, however, the script does not seem to have been finalized in advance, since there was no agreed-upon location where the mass killing was supposed to take place. Józef Chrzanowski testified to this: "When I came to the square, they [Sobuta and Wasilewski] told me to give my barn to burn the jews. But I started pleading to spare my barn, to which they agreed and left my barn in peace, only told me to help them chase the jews to Bronisław Śleszyński's barn."[17]

The murderers were determined to take away their victims' dignity before they took their lives. "I saw how Sobuta and Wasilewski took some dozen Jews from among the assembled and ordered them to do some ridiculous gymnastics exercises."[18] Before the Jews were chased along on their last brief journey from the square to the barn where they would all perish, Sobuta and his colleagues organized a sideshow. During the Soviet occupation a statue of Lenin had been erected in town, right next to the main square. So "a group of Jews was brought to the little square to fell Lenin's statue. When Jews broke the statue, they were told to put its various pieces on some boards and carry it around, and the rabbi was told to walk in front with his hat on a stick, and all had to sing, 'The war is because of us, the war is for us.' While carrying the statue all the Jews were chased toward the barn, and the barn was doused with gasoline and lit, and in this manner fifteen hundred Jewish people perished."[19]

In the immediate vicinity of the barn, as we remember, a thick crowd was milling, helping to shove the beaten, wounded, and terrorized Jews inside. "We chased jews under the barn," Jerzy Laudański would later report, "and we ordered them to enter inside, and the jews had to enter inside."[20]

From the inside of the barn we are told two stories. One concerns Michał Kuropatwa, a coachman, who some time earlier had helped a Polish army officer hide from his Soviet pursuers. When the self-styled leaders of the pogrom noticed him in the Jewish crowd, he was taken out and told that because he had helped a Polish officer earlier, he might now go home. But he refused, choosing to share the fate of his people.[21]

The barn was then doused with kerosene, issued at the warehouse by Antoni Niebrzydowski to his brother Jerzy and Eugeniusz Kalinowski. "They brought the eight liters of kerosene that I had issued to them and doused the barn filled with Jews and lit it up; what followed I do not know."[22] But we do know—the Jews were burned alive. At the last moment Janek Neumark managed to tear himself away from this hell. A surge of hot air must have blown the barn door open. He was standing right next to it with his sister and her five-year-old daughter. Staszek Sielawa barred their exit, wielding an ax. But Neumark wrestled it away from him and they managed to run away and hide in the cemetery. The last thing he remembered from inside was the sight of his father, already engulfed in flames.[23]

The fire must have spread unevenly. It appears to have moved from east to west, perhaps on account of the wind. Afterward, in the east wing of the incinerated building a few charred corpses could be found; there were some more in the center, and toward the western end a multitude of the dead were piled up. The bodies in the upper layer of the heap had been consumed by fire, but those beneath had been crushed and asphyxiated, their clothes in many cases remaining intact. "They were so intertwined with one another that bodies could not be disentangled," recalled an elderly peasant who, as a young boy, had been sent with a group of local men to bury the dead. And he added a detail in unwitting confirmation of Wasersztajn's chilling testimony: "In spite of this people were trying to search the corpses, looking for valuables sewn into clothing. I touched a Brolin shoe-polish box. It clinked. I cut it through with a shovel, and some coins glittered—I think golden tzarist five-ruble coins. People jumped over to collect them, and this drew the attention of onlooking gendarmes. They searched everybody. And if someone put the find in his pocket, they took it away and gave him a good shove. But anyone who hid it in his shoe saved the catch."[24]

The worst murderer of the whole lot was probably a certain Kobrzyniecki. We are also told by some witnesses that he was the one who ignited the barn. "Later people said that the most jews were killed by citizen Kobrzyniecki—I don't know his first name," recalls witness Edward Śleszyński, in whose father's barn most of Jedwabne's Jews were killed on that day. "He apparently personally killed eighteen jews and participated the most in the burning of the barn."[25] Housewife Aleksandra Karwowska knew from Kobrzyniecki himself that he had "knifed to death eighteen jews. He said this in my apartment when he was putting up the stove."[26]

It was the middle of a very hot July, and the burned and asphyxiated corpses of murder victims had to be buried quickly. But there were no more Jews in town who could be ordered to accomplish this grisly task. "Late in the evening," recalls Wincenty Gościcki, "I was taken by the germans to bury those burned corpses. But I could not do this because when I saw this, I started to vomit and I was released from burying the cadavers."[27] Apparently he was not the only one who couldn't stomach the job, since "on the second or the third day after the murder," we are told once again by Bardoń, "I was standing with Mayor Karolak in the square not far from the outpost, and the commander of the outpost of the German gendarmerie in Jedwabne, Adamy, came up and said to the mayor with emphasis, So, kill people and burn them you managed, eh? but bury them no one is eager to, eh? by morning, all must be buried! Understood?"[28] This angry outburst by the local gendarmerie commander quickly became the talk of the town. Sixty years later Leon Dziedzic from Przestrzele near Jedwabne could still quote his words: " 'You insisted that you'd put things in order with the Jews [*że zrobicie porządek z Żydami*], but you don't know how to put things in order at all.' He [the German gendarme] was afraid that an epidemic might break out because it was very hot and dogs were already getting at [the corpses]."[29] But this was an "impossible job," as Leon Dziedzic further clarified in another interview. For the piled-up bodies of Jewish victims were entwined with one another "as roots of a tree.' Somebody hit upon the idea that we should tear them into pieces and throw these pieces into the dugout. They brought pitchforks, and we tore the bodies as best we could: here a head, there a leg."[30]

After July 10th, Poles were no longer permitted to kill the Jews of Jedwabne at will. The routine of the German occupation administration was reestablished. A few survivors returned to town. They lingered there for a while—a few worked at the gendarmerie outpost—and in the end they were driven by the Nazis to the ghetto in Łomża. About a dozen people survived the war. Seven of the total had been hidden and cared for in the nearby Janczewo hamlet, by the Wyrzykowski family.

P LUNDER

One big subject is omitted from the sources and testimonies at our disposal. What happened to the property of the Jedwabne Jews? Those Jews who survived the war knew that they had lost everything. As to who took over the property, or how it was disposed of, this is not a subject they address in their memorial book. During interrogations in the 1949 and 1953 trials, neither the witnesses nor the accused were asked questions about this either. So we are left with but a few bits and pieces of information.

According to Eliasz Grądowski the following people grabbed Jewish property during and after the pogrom: Gienek Kozłowski,

Józef Sobuta, Rozalia Śleszyńska, and Józef Chrzanowski. Julia Sokołowska adds to this list the names of Karol Bardoń, Fredek Stefany, Kazimierz Karwowski, and the two Kobrzenieckis. Abram Boruszczak says the same about the Laudański brothers and Anna Polkowska.[1] But all this testimony lacks specific details and makes only vague allusions to the appropriation of Jewish property by perpetrators of the pogrom. Józef Sobuta's wife, Stanisława, provided more concrete information when she explained during her husband's trial that they had "moved into a 'leftover' Jewish dwelling [the house of the Stern family] at the request of the surviving son of the owner, who had been killed, because he was afraid to live there alone."[2] Witness Sulewski states that he "does not know" who gave permission to the Sobuta couple to take over a Jewish house, and then adds, "As far as I know leftover Jewish dwellings could be taken over without anybody's permission."[3]

This strikes me as a rather naive, if not disingenuous, view of the matter; and, in fact, the wife of Stanisław Sielawa gives a more general aperçu of the "leftover" Jewish property question, which suggests that the same people who had organized the pogrom afterward took charge of Jewish property as well (recall that both Wasersztajn's and Neumark's depositions name the Sielawa brothers among the most active participants of the pogrom). "I heard from the local people, but I don't remember from whom exactly, that Sobuta Józef with the mayor of Jedwabne, Karolak, after the murder of the Jews of Jedwabne [the phrase used in the deposition—*po wymordowaniu Żydów w Jedwabnym*—could just as well be translated as "after having murdered the Jews of Jedwabne"] participated in transporting the leftover Jewish property to some warehouse, but I do not know exactly how this transporting was done, and I also don't know whether Sobuta Józef took for himself some of the leftover Jewish property."[4] During her court appearance she gets even more specific: "I saw how they transported Jewish things, but the accused [i.e., Sobuta] only stood next to the horse cart with things, and I do not know whether the accused *belonged to this business* [my emphasis; *czy oskarżony należał do tego interesu*]."[5]

A few words might be in order here once again about the Śleszyńskis' barn. On January

11, 1949—that is, immediately after the wave of arrests swept through town—the Łomża Security Office (UB) received a letter from a certain Henryk Krystowczyk. He was using the opportunity created by the opening of an investigation into the massacre of Jedwabne Jews, Krystowczyk wrote, to raise another issue: "In April 1945 my brother Zygmunt Krystowczyk was assassinated, because as a member of the PPR [Polish Workers' Party—this was the name that the Polish Communist Party bore at the time] he was ordered to organize a ZSCh [a peasant cooperative]—a task he accomplished. Then he was elected chairman of the cooperative. While he was chairman of the ZSCh, he began renovation of a steam mill near Przystrzelska Street, a leftover Jewish property." Krystowczyk proceeds to describe the circumstances of his brother's murder, who was involved in it, and how the culprit wanted to take over the mill. He explains that the building materials used for renovation were provided by his brother, who was a carpenter by profession. "The wood for renovation came from the barn of citizen Bronisław Śleszyński, which we took down because the Germans had built it for him to replace the old barn, which he gave voluntarily to kill the Jews, and which burned down together with the Jews."[6]

Thus, as we see, the so-called leftover Jewish property remained a hotly contested issue in town, involving assassinations and denunciations to the Security Office, as late as 1949. It shows up in several documents of the secret police at the time. The original denunciation reporting the sighting of Mayor Karolak after the war on a Warsaw street contains the statement "He was arrested by the German authorities, as far as I know, because of all the riches he took from the jews and did not divide equally with the germans." In another anonymous denunciation concerning various dealings of the Laudański family, the informant asserts that Jerzy Laudański was arrested by the Germans while he was trying to smuggle jewelry robbed from the Jews. It also describes how another Laudański, after the war, ostentatiously wore an elegant "Jewish" fur coat.[7] All of this should not surprise us, since the effects of the Jedwabne Jews' incineration were not unlike those of a neutron bomb dropped on some community: all the owners were eliminated, while their property remained intact.

And thus it must have been a very profitable "business," indeed, for those who managed to lay their hands on it.

Given our growing awareness of the importance of material expropriation as a motivating factor in the persecution of the Jews all over Europe, I would think it very probable that the desire and unexpected opportunity to rob the Jews once and for all—rather than, or alongside with, atavistic antisemitism—was the real motivating force that drove Karolak and his cohort to organize the killing. Half a century after the massacre, people of Jedwabne, apparently, think likewise: "In Jedwabne everybody knew the truth [about the murder of the Jews], but people did not previously speak about it publicly. On Saturday, May 13, [2000], during a mass for the fatherland, the local priest called on parishioners to pray also for those victims of war who lost their lives because of the boundless, criminal desire of some people to enrich themselves."[8]

INTIMATE BIOGRAPHIES

In addition to protocols of interrogation of the witnesses and the accused we find, in the court files of Ramotowski and his associates, many other documents that were presented to the judicial authorities at different stages of the proceedings. I quoted earlier from the clemency petition filed by Karol Bardoń, for example. My initial assessment leading to the conclusion that these were a "bunch of ordinary men" was based largely on information culled from the first page of each protocol. But we can tell more about the accused than simply their ages, how many children they sired, and what they did for a living.

A few days after the initial arrests in January 1949, wives of the arrested men started sending petitions to the Łomża Security Office laying out the special circumstances that, they hoped, would cast a better light on their husbands' role during the anti-Jewish pogrom. We can tease out from these texts interesting biographical details about the accused. Thus Irena Janowska, the wife of Aleksander, writes on January 28 that "on the critical day German gendarmerie walked around together with the mayor and the secretary [of the town council] Wasilewski, and chased out males to go and guard Jews who were assembled in the square. They came to my house as well, where they found my husband, and ordered him sternly, threatening with a gun, to go to the square. My husband was afraid, did not know exactly what was going on, and feared for himself because under the first Soviets he worked as an inspector in a milk cooperative."[1] Three days later Janina Żyluk writes a petition on behalf of her arrested husband (named by many witnesses as one of the main perpetrators): "My husband, until the Soviet-German war broke out in 1941, worked as a supervisor in tax collection. For this reason after the Germans came in 1941 he had to hide, because every-body who worked for the Soviets was pursued and persecuted."[2]

We know that state bureaucracy vastly ex-panded under the Soviet administration, and that people had to make a living, and many therefore worked for the occupiers. Also, it may have seemed logical to a wife of a man arrested by Stalinist security police that his lot would improve when it came to be known that he had once worked for a Soviet administra-tion. So I would not attribute to these two bio-graphical snippets more than curiosity value were it not for the fact that there were addi-tional revelations of this sort in the files. And they kept getting more and more interesting. Take, for instance, this confessional text by Karol Bardoń—the only man who received a death sentence in Ramotowski's case:

Following the Red Army's entrance into the Bia-łystok voivodeship, and after Soviet authorities were established in October of 1939, I returned to mending clocks, and occasionally, until April 20, 1940, I also carried out various commissioned jobs in my field of expertise for the NKVD and other Offices of Soviet Authorities [capitals in original]. *Here I was opening safes because keys were missing; I changed locks, made new keys, repaired typewriters, etc. On April 20, 1940, I became a supervisor* [majster] *as a mechanic and head of the repair shop at the MTS* [Mechanical Tractor Station]. *I repaired tractors on wheels and on tracks, agricultural machinery, as well as cars for various kolkhozes and sovkhozes. In this mechanical center I was a brigade leader of the first brigade and a technical controller. At the same time I was a deputy to the city soviet* [gorsoviet] *of the town of Jedwabne in Łomża County.*[3]

Bardoń was evidently a very good mechanic. But no professional qualifications would, by themselves, put him into all these positions under the Soviets. Clearly, he was also a trusted man.

And there is, finally, the *pièce de résistance*: an autobiographical revelation from one of the greatest evildoers on that day, the older Laudański brother, Zygmunt. This is what he wrote in a petition addressed to "the Ministry of Justice at the Security Police Office in Warsaw [*Do Ministerstwa Sprawiedliwości U.B.P. w Warszawie*]" from his jail in Ostrowiec on July 4, 1949:

When our territory was incorporated into the BSSR [Belorussian Soviet Socialist Republic] *I was hiding at the time for about six months from the Soviet authorities. . . . While I was hiding from deportation, I did not join bands of outlaws that were forming at the time on our territory, but I sent a plea to Generalissimus Stalin, which was forwarded by Moscow's prosecutor's office, Puszkinska Street 15, to the NKVD office in Jedwabne with an order to review. After I was questioned and investigated, it turned out that I had been unjustly punished, and in order to recover my losses I was allowed to come out of hiding, free of the threat of deportation. After observing my views, the NKVD in Jedwabne called me to join in work at liquidating anti-Soviet evil.* [It looks as though Laudański might have been one of the *pentiti* of NKVD colonel Misiuriew.] *At that time I made contact with the NKVD in Jedwabne (I do not state my pseudonym in writing). During my contact, in order to make my work more effective, my superiors ordered me (in order to avoid detection by reactionary elements) to take an anti-Soviet attitude, since I was already known by the authorities. When suddenly the Soviet-german* [capital and lowercase letter in original] *war broke out in*

1941, the NKVD did not manage to destroy all its documents, and I was afraid and did not go out, and only surreptitiously did I establish [by sending his younger brother to work in the German gendarmerie right away!] *that the most important documents were burned in the NKVD courtyard. . . . I feel wronged by the entire sentence, because my views are different from what is suspected, because when I was in contact with the NKVD, my life was permanently in danger. And now* [i.e., after the war] *I did not join any reactionary bands but left my hometown and started working in the gmina Cooperative of Peasant Self-Help, which was persecuted by reactionaries. By joining the Polish Workers' Party, I felt how my well-being improved in the Democratic spirit, and* I believe that on shoulders like mine our workers' regime may safely rest [my emphasis]. *I declare that only as a misunderstood man I ended up in jail, because if my opinion about friendship with the Soviet Union had been known, then reactionary bands, if not the germans, would have destroyed me together with my family.*[4]

We are struck at the first reading of this exposé by the unbending conformism of this man. Apparently, he tried to anticipate what each successive carnivorous regime of this epoch might most desire of its subjects, and went to extremes in his zeal to please—first by becoming a secret NKVD collaborator, then by doing the Nazis' dirty work in killing the Jews, and finally by joining the Communist Party, the PPR. The French have a good expression to describe this mode of adaptation to changing circumstances, a race with destiny called *fuite en avant*.

But these scraps of biographies of four individuals who turned out to have been collaborators with the Soviet authorities before they became German collaborators (in addition to killing the Jews in the pogrom, two among the accused—Jerzy Laudański and Karol Bardoń—would later join the German gendarmerie) point to a more general phenomenon, I believe, than the mere individual trajectories of a few evil men. It is not just a question of character that plays itself out in this drama, but also the logic of incentives one encounters within the totalitarian regimes of the twentieth century. I shall comment on this issue in concluding remarks, for I see here interpretive possibilities of wartime and postwar Polish history that have not yet been fully explored.

In the meantime, I want to conclude this close encounter with Jedwabne antiheroes with a *cri de coeur* of the youngest Laudański, Jerzy, who by all accounts was the worst murderer among the accused. He must have been a strapping youth, six feet tall, and full of energy. In the control-investigative files of the Stalinist secret police, where all defendants were characterized according to thirty-four different traits, under the rubric "speech" Laudański's is described as "Loud, Clear, Polish." Other fellow accused's speech is mostly characterized as "Quiet."[5] In 1956, as the last of all the Łomża trial defendants still in prison, he sends out a plea. In a shameless display of moral idiocy, he asks, Why do you keep me behind bars if I was not a German sympathizer but rather a true Polish patriot?

Since I was raised in an area of intense struggles against the Jews, and during the war Germans mass-murdered Jews over there, also in other localities, why me, the youngest in the trial and raised [in Poland] *during the Sanacja period* [i.e., before the war], *why should I be the only*

*one treated with full severity of the law? After
all, since the school bench I was taught only in one
direction, which means that during the occupation I was preoccupied only with matters related
to my Nation and my Motherland. As a proof of
it, I did not hesitate when there was need to give
my strengths for the good of the Motherland during the occupation. I went underground and
joined a conspiratorial organization by the name
Polish Association for Insurrection* [Polski Zwią-
zek Powstańczy, in its later incarnation, the
Home Army, AK] *to fight against the occupier
in autumn of 1941 in Poręba, by the river Bug
in Ostrów Mazowiecki County, and my activity
there was to transport underground newspapers
and other items. In May of 1942 the gestapo arrested me and I was imprisoned in Pawiak* [the
main prison in Warsaw] *and then deported to
concentration camps, Auschwitz, Gross-Rosen,
Oranienburg, where I suffered for three years
alongside others as a Pole and a political prisoner.
And after the Red Army liberated us in 1945, I
did not follow those who abandoned their devastated Motherland and preferred easy western life
only to return later, but as spies or wreckers.
Without a moment of hesitation I returned to the
devastated Country, to my Nation, to whom I*

offered my young, just barely twenty-year-old life, in the struggle against the occupier. The court, however, did not take under consideration my above proofs that I was in no way a supporter of the occupier, and certainly not like one the Security Office in Łomża made of me in the investigation on the basis of which I received such a long sentence. After returning [to Poland] I worked all the time in state institutions.[6]

In some perverse way this man was making a valid point, though. After all, he was sentenced under a paragraph that penalized not so much concrete deeds as the fact of collaboration with the Germans. And, of course, in his own mind he had not been collaborating with any occupiers. He was a regular guy, a good patriot acting in collaboration, at most, with his own neighbors. Jerzy Laudański was released on parole, the last among the condemned in this trial, on February 18, 1957.[7]

In Jedwabne ordinary Poles slaughtered the Jews, very much as ordinary Germans from the *Ordnungspolizei* Batallion no. 101 did in Jozefów, as documented in Christopher Browning's *Ordinary Men.* They were men of all ages and of different professions; entire families on occasion, fathers and sons acting in concert; good citizens, one is tempted to say (if sarcasm were not out of place, given the hideousness of their deeds), who heeded the call of municipal authorities. And what the Jews saw, to their horror and, I dare say, incomprehension, were familiar faces. Not anonymous men in uniform, cogs in a war machine, agents carrying out orders, but their own neighbors, who chose to kill and were engaged in a bloody pogrom—willing executioners.

ANACHRONISM

The massacre of Jedwabne Jews leaves a historian of modern Poland perplexed and groping for explanation. Nothing of the sort has been recorded or written about in scholarly literature. In a desperate effort to somehow domesticate these events, images from the distant past flood memory, giving the semblance (by virtue of familiarity) of making sense of what we have learned. Perhaps the mass murders in Radziłów and Jedwabne were an anachronism belonging to an entirely different epoch? One cannot shake the impression that by some evil magic peasant mobs stepped off the pages of Henryk Sienkiewicz's national saga of seventeenth-century wars,

Trilogy, onto the soil of Białystok voivodeship in the summer of 1941. Ever since Khmielnicki's peasant wars (which in Jewish mythologized memory are encoded by the terrifying word *Khurban*, catastrophe, a foreshadowing of the Shoah), Jews had suffered the destructive force inimical to everything different that lay in wait in the countryside of those lands, bursting into the open, occasionally, in paroxysms of violence. Evidently, *rzeź i rabacja* (slaughter and plunder) remained in the standing repertory of collective behavior in these parts and was played out every so often during the nineteenth and twentieth centuries.[1]

Where did this explosive potential come from? We must remember that in the background of anti-Jewish violence there always lurked a suspicion of ritual murder, a conviction that Jews use for the preparation of Passover matzoh the fresh blood of innocent Christian children. It was a deeply ingrained belief among many Polish Catholics, and not simply among residents of the boondocks. After all, rumors that Jews were engaging in these practices drew incensed crowds into the streets of Polish *cities* at a moment's notice even after the Second World War. This was the mechanism that triggered the most infamous postwar pogroms, in Cracow in 1945 and in Kielce in 1946.[2] And nothing could frighten activists of Jewish Committees, or Jewish survivors after the war, more than a visit to their neighborhood from a concerned Christian parent looking around for a missing child![3]

The Shoah has been portrayed in scholarly literature as a phenomenon rooted in modernity. We know very well that in order to kill millions of people, an efficient bureaucracy is necessary, along with a (relatively) advanced technology. But the murder of Jedwabne Jews reveals yet another, deeper, more archaic layer of this enterprise. I am referring not only to the motivations of the murderers—after all, Jedwabne residents and peasants from Łomża County could not yet have managed to soak up the vicious anti-Jewish Nazi propaganda, even if they had been willing and ready—but also to primitive, ancient methods and murder weapons: stones, wooden clubs, iron bars, fire, and water; as well as the absence of organization. It is clear, from what happened in Jedwabne, that we must approach the Holocaust as a heterogeneous phenomenon. On the one hand, we have to be able to account for it as a system, which functioned according to a pre-conceived (though constantly evolving) plan. But, simultaneously, we must also be able to see it as a mosaic composed of discrete episodes, improvised by local decision-makers, and hinging on unforced behavior, rooted in God-knows-what motivations, of all those who were near the murder scene at the time. This makes all the difference in terms of assessing responsibility for the killings, as well as calculating the odds for survival that confronted the Jews.

WHAT DO PEOPLE REMEMBER?

One of the premier authors of modern Hebrew literature, Aharon Appelfeld, returned in 1996 to his native village near Czernovitz, where he had spent the first eight and a half years of his life, untill June 1941. "What does a child of eight and a half remember? Almost nothing. But, miraculously, that 'almost nothing' has nourished me for years. Not a day passes when I'm not at home. In my adopted country of Israel, I have written thirty books that draw directly or indirectly upon the village of my childhood, whose name is found only on ordinance maps. That 'almost nothing' is the well from which I draw and draw, and it seems that there is no end to its waters."

And so when he returned fifty years later, the beauty and odd familiarity of the landscape once again evoked a sense of well-being and careless joy. "Who could imagine that in this village, on a Saturday, our Sabbath, sixty-two souls, most of them women and children, would fall prey to pitchforks and kitchen knives, and I, because I was in a back room, would manage to escape to the cornfields and hide?"[1]

Appelfeld had come to the village with his wife and a film crew that was recording his return to the native village. A group of local people gathered to look the strangers over; when Appelfeld asked about the burial site of the Jews who were murdered during the war, it seemed that no one could give him an answer. But after a time it emerged that he had lived there as a child, and then someone who had gone to school with him recognized him. Eventually "a tall peasant came up, and, as if in an old ceremony, the village people explained to him what I wanted to know. He raised his arm and pointed: it was over there, on a hill. There was silence, then an outpouring of speech, which I could not understand."

Appelfeld continues, "It turned out that what the people of the village had tried to conceal from me was well known, even to the children. I asked several little children, who were standing near the fence and looking at us, where the Jews' graves were. Right away, they raised their hands and pointed." And they all went toward that hill, not speaking much along the way, until "finally one of them said, 'Here is the grave.' He pointed at an uncultivated field. 'Are you sure?' I asked. 'I buried them,' the peasant replied. He added, 'I was sixteen.' "[2]

Just as Appelfeld found his mother's grave half a century after her violent death in his native village, another writer, Henryk Grynberg in Poland, found the skeleton of his father, killed in the spring of 1944, near the place where the family had hidden at the time. Local villagers knew very well who had murdered Grynberg, when and for what reason, as well as where the body was buried. Polish film audiences could see the whole story unfold as a handheld camera followed Grynberg's quest for his father's grave in the prizewinning documentary by Paweł Łoziński called *The Place of Birth*. And of course the entire population of Jedwabne knows very well what took place in their town on July 10, 1941.

That is why I believe that detailed recollections of this epoch are preserved in every town and village where Jews were murdered. And this is as it should be—for those who witnessed such a horrible tragedy would be callous indeed if they had all but forgotten what happened. But this is also a curse—for not infrequently the local population did not merely witness the murder of their Jewish neighbors but were actively involved in the killing. How can we otherwise explain why after the war the Gentiles who had offered assistance to Jews at the risk of their own lives—Gentiles who were later recognized by the Yad Vashem authority as the Righteous Amongst Nations—as a rule feared revealing before their neighbors that they had hidden Jews under the German occupation?[3]

That they had ample reasons to be afraid we can learn from the people whose lives are forever connected to the history of Jedwabne Jews. I will not recount the full story of how the Wyrzykowski family managed to save

Wasersztajn and six other Jews during the occupation. But what happened to them *after* the liberation does pertain to our topic.

I, Aleksander Wyrzykowski, together with my wife Antonia, we wanted to make the following deposition. When the Red Army came, these martyrs were free; we dressed them up as best we could. The first one went to his house, but his family had perished so he came to eat with us. The rest went to their places. One Sunday I noticed that guerrillas[4] were coming and they said, We'll come over today and get rid of the Jew, and the other said that they would kill everybody one night. From this time on the Jew slept in the field in a dugout for potatoes; I gave him a pillow and my coat. I went to warn the others as well. They started to hide. The two girls who were their fiancées the guerrillas had nothing against, and those bandits told them not to say a word to their fiancés that they came. This same night they came to us to get the Jew; they said to give him away, that they would kill him and would no longer bother us. My wife replied that I had gone to visit my sister, and that the Jew had gone to Łomża and hadn't come back. Then they started to beat her so that she didn't have a white patch

on her body, only black skin everywhere. They
took what good things they found in the house
and told her to drive them back. My wife took
them in a horse cart near to Jedwabne. When she
returned, the Jew came out of the hiding place
and saw how she was beaten up. After a certain
time another Jew, Janek Kubrzański, came. We
talked afterward and decided to run away from
this place. We took residence in Łomża. My wife
left a little child with her parents. From Łomża
we moved to Białystok, because we feared for our
lives. . . . In 1946 we moved to Bielsk Podlaski.
But after a few years this was found out, and we
had to leave Bielsk Podlaski.

So the stigma of having helped Jews during
the occupation stuck to the Wyrzykowski
family for good, and it followed them from
place to place and, as it turned out, also from
generation to generation.[5] Antonia Wyrzykowska in the end escaped across the ocean
and settled in Chicago. The son of Antonia
Wyrzykowska's nephew, who remained near
Jedwabne, was called "a Jew" whenever his
playmates got angry.

COLLECTIVE RESPONSIBILITY

Even though the Nazi-conceived project of the eradication of world Jewry will remain, at its core, a mystery, we know a lot about various mechanisms of the "final solution." And one of the things we do know is that the *Einsatz-gruppen*, German police detachments, and various functionaries who implemented the "final solution" did not compel the local population to participate directly in the murder of Jews. Bloody pogroms were tolerated, sometimes even invited, especially after the opening of the Russo-German war—a special directive was issued to this effect by the head of the Main Reich Security Office, Reinhardt Heydrich.[1] A lot of prohibitions concerning the

Jews were issued as well. In occupied Poland, for example, people could not, under penalty of death, offer assistance to Jews hiding outside of the German-designated ghettos. Though there were sadistic individuals who, particularly in camps, might force prisoners to kill each other, in general nobody was forced to kill the Jews. In other words, *the so-called local population involved in killings of Jews did so of its own free will*.

And if in collective Jewish memory this phenomenon is ingrained—that local Polish people killed the Jews because they wanted to, not because they had to—then Jews will hold them to be particularly responsible for what they have done. A murderer in uniform remains a state functionary acting under orders, and he might even be presumed to have mental reservations about what he has been ordered to do. Not so a civilian, killing another human being of his own free will—such an evildoer is unequivocally but a murderer.

Poles hurt the Jews in numerous interactions throughout the war. And it is not exclusively killings that are stressed in people's recollections from the period. One might recall, for illustration, a few women described in an autobiographical fragment, "A Quarter-Hour Passed in a Pastry Shop," from a powerful memoir by Michał Głowiński, today one of the foremost literary critics in Poland. He was a little boy at the time of the German occupation. On this occasion an aunt had left him alone for fifteen minutes in a little Warsaw café; after sitting him down at a table with a pastry, she went out to make a few telephone calls. As soon as she left the premises, the young Jewish boy became an object of scrutiny and questioning by a flock of women who could just as well have left him in peace.[2] Between this episode and the Jedwabne murders one can inscribe an entire range of Polish-Jewish encounters that, in the midst of all their situational variety, had one feature in common: they all carried potentially deadly consequences for the Jews.

When reflecting about this epoch, we must not assign collective responsibility. We must be clearheaded enough to remember that for each killing only a specific murderer or group of murderers is responsible. But we nevertheless might be compelled to investigate what makes a nation (as in "the Germans") capable of carrying out such deeds. Or can atrocious deeds simply be bracketed off and forgotten? Can we arbitrarily select from a national heritage what we like, and proclaim it as patrimony to the exclusion of everything else? Or just the opposite: if people are indeed bonded together by authentic spiritual affinity—I have in mind a kind of national pride rooted in common historical experiences of many generations—are they not somehow responsible also for horrible deeds perpetrated by members of such an "imagined community"? Can a young German reflecting today on the meaning of his identity as a German simply ignore twelve years (1933–1945) of his country's and his ancestors' history?

And even if selectivity in the process of forging national identity is unavoidable (one cannot write "everything" into one's own self-image, if only because nobody knows "everything," and, in any case, even with the best intentions it would be next to impossible to have a global recall), the boundaries of a collective identity so constructed—in order to remain *authentic*—would have to remain open forever. Anyone must be at any time empowered to challenge such a construct by asking how some episode, or series of episodes, or an epoch from ancestral history, fits into the proposed self-image of a nation.

Usually the canon of collective identity is assembled from deeds that are somehow special, striking, or remarkable. It is made up, in other words, of actions that depart from routine, that are unusual. And even though it is only a Fryderyk, a Jan, or a Mikołaj who has actually performed such deeds, as constitutive components of the canon they also belong to the collective "us." Hence Polish music, most deservedly, is proud of "our" Chopin; Polish science of "our" Copernicus; and Poland thinks of itself as a "bastion of Christianity [*przedmurze chrześcijaństwa*])" in no small part because King Jan Sobieski defeated the Turks in an important battle near Vienna. For this reason we are entitled to ask whether deeds committed by the likes of Laudański and Karolak—since they were so striking and unusual—engage Polish collective identity as well.

My question is, of course, rhetorical, because we understand very well that such a mass murder affects all in a community across time. It is enough to recall a vocal public discussion that was triggered by an article published in the largest Polish daily, *Gazeta Wyborcza*, by Michał Cichy, in which he discussed the murder of several Jews in Warsaw during the Warsaw Uprising, in the summer of 1944, committed by a Polish Home Army detachment.[3] The spirited public reaction evidenced by the many letters sent to the editors after publication manifests how strongly such odious behavior by a group of demoralized young men engages Poles half a century later. What of the Jedwabne massacre, then, which dwarfs anything we previously imagined concerning the criminal aspect of Polish-Jewish relations during the war?

NEW APPROACH TO SOURCES

The mass murder of Jedwabne Jews in the summer of 1941 opens up historiography of Polish-Jewish relations during the Second World War. Sedatives that were administered in connection with this subject by historians and journalists for over fifty years have to be put aside. It is simply not true that Jews were murdered in Poland during the war solely by the Germans, occasionally assisted in the execution of their gruesome task by some auxiliary police formations composed primarily of Latvians, Ukrainians, or some other "Kalmuks," not to mention the proverbial "fall guys" whom everybody castigated because it was so easy not to take responsibility for what they had done—the so-called *szmalcowniks*, extortionists who made a profession of blackmailing Jews trying to pass and survive in hiding. By singling them out as culprits, historians and others have found it easy to bring closure to the matter by saying that there is "scum" in every society, that these were a few "socially marginal" individuals, and that they were dealt with by underground courts anyway.[1]

After Jedwabne the issue of Polish-Jewish relations during the war can no longer be put to rest with such ready-made formulas. Indeed, we have to rethink not only wartime but also postwar Polish history, as well as reevaluate certain important interpretive themes widely accepted as explanations accounting for outcomes, attitudes, and institutions of those years.

To begin with, I suggest that we should modify our approach to sources for this period. When considering survivors' testimonies, we would be well advised to change the starting premise in appraisal of their evidentiary contribution from a priori critical to in principle affirmative. By accepting what we read in a particular account as fact *until we find persuasive arguments to the contrary*, we would avoid more mistakes than we are likely to commit by adopting the opposite approach, which calls for cautious skepticism toward any testimony *until an independent confirmation of its content has been found.* The greater the catastrophe the fewer the survivors. We must be capable of listening to lonely voices reaching us from the abyss, as did Wasersztajn's testimony before the memorial book of Jedwabne Jews was published, or such as still remains, as best I can tell, Finkelsztajn's testimony about the destruction of the Jewish community in Radziłów.

I make the point, to some extent, on the basis of my own experience. It took me four years, as I stated at the beginning of this volume, to understand what Wasersztajn was communicating in his deposition. But the same conclusion—that we ought to accept as true Jewish testimonies about atrocities committed by the local population until they are proven false—suggests itself as we consider the general absence in Polish historiography of any studies about the involvement of the ethnically Polish population in the destruction of Polish Jewry. It is a subject of fundamental

importance that has been extremely well documented. In the Jewish Historical Institute in
Warsaw alone one can find over seven thousand depositions collected from the survivors
of the Holocaust immediately after the war,
which provide voluminous evidence of collu-
sion by the Poles in the destruction of their
Jewish neighbors. But quite often—as with
Wasersztajn's and Finkelsztajn's testimony—
these come from the only surviving witnesses,
who have utterly "incredible" stories to tell.
All I am arguing for is the suspension of our
incredulity.

But, in the last analysis, it is not our professional inadequacy (as a community of historians of this period) that calls most compel-
lingly for revision in the approach to sources.
This methodological imperative follows from
the very immanent character of all evidence
about the destruction of Polish Jewry that we
are ever likely to come across.

All that we know about the Holocaust—by
virtue of the fact that it has been told—is not
a representative sample of the Jewish fate suffered under Nazi rule. It is all skewed evidence, biased in one direction: these are all
stories with a happy ending. They have all

been produced by a few who were lucky enough to survive. Even statements from witnesses who have not survived—statements that have been interrupted by the sudden death of their authors, who therefore left only fragments of what they wanted to say—belong to this category. For what has reached us was written only while the authors were still alive. About the "heart of darkness" that was also the very essence of their experience, about their last betrayal, about the Calvary of 90 percent of the prewar Polish Jewry—we will never know. And that is why we must take literally all fragments of information at our disposal, fully aware that what actually happened to the Jewish community during the Holocaust can only be more tragic than the existing representation of events based on surviving evidence.

Is IT POSSIBLE TO BE SIMULTANEOUSLY A VICTIM AND A VICTIMIZER?

War is a myth-creating experience in the life of every society. But in Eastern, Central, and Southern Europe it is continuously a source of vivid, only too often lethal, legitimization narratives. The memory, indeed the symbolism, of collective, national martyrology during the Second World War is paramount for the self-understanding of Polish society in the twentieth century.[1] Every town has its sacred sites commemorating victims of terror; every family its horror stories of executions, imprisonment, and deportation. How can we fit the unvarnished history of Polish-Jewish relations during the war into this picture? After all, Jedwabne—though perhaps one of the most excessive (*the* most excessive, it must be hoped) of all murderous assaults by Poles against the Jews—was not an isolated episode. And it prompts us to ask a question: can one, as a group with a distinctive collective identity, be at the same time a victim and a perpetrator? Is it possible to suffer and inflict suffering at the same time?

In the postmodern world the answer to such questions is very simple—of course it is possible. Furthermore, such an answer has already been given with reference to collective experiences during the Second World War. When the Allies finally occupied Germany and "discovered" concentration camps, they made an effort to confront every German with knowledge of Nazi crimes as part of their denazification campaign. The response of German public opinion was rather unexpected: *Armes Deutschland*, "Poor Germany."[2] This was how news of German crimes perpetrated during the war resonated within German society: the world will hate us for what the Nazis have done. It was apparently easy for the Germans to take on a sense of victimization since it alleviated, in a manner of speaking, the burden of responsibility for the war and suffering inflicted on countless victims.

But such an overlay of contradictory narratives usually generates conflict and debate. We might for illustration take note of a protracted public controversy sparked in Germany by a photographic exhibition about the German army's role in genocide (*Vernichtungskrieg. Verbrechen der Wehrmacht 1941 bis 1944*), mounted by the Hamburg Institute for Social Research. The regular army, where any German male of draft age might have served, was not supposed to have been involved in the atrocities committed against the Jews (according to the prevailing consensus). Of course German historians knew that the army had participated in atrocities, and wrote accordingly. Nevertheless, the wider public was not ready to accept evidence that ran counter to this deeply held conviction. Will acceptance of responsibility for odious deeds perpetrated during World War II—on top of a deeply ingrained, and well-deserved, sense of victimization suffered at the time—come easily and naturally to the Polish public?

Jews who found themselves in DP camps in Germany after the war—as we know, some

200,000 Jews fled from Poland after 1945, mostly to these camps—used to say that Germans would never forgive the Jews for what they had done to them. One wonders whether the same formula would not be a better explanation of postwar Polish antisemitism than the usually invoked Jewish names of prominent Communist leaders from the Stalinist era (typically Berman and Minc),[3] whose nefarious deeds supposedly induced such general negative attitudes toward the Jews among the Polish public.

Antipathy toward the Jews in Poland after the war was widespread and full of aggression, and one would be hard-pressed to demonstrate that it resulted from a cool and detached analysis of the postwar political situation prevailing in the country. And one need not base this assessment on conversations reported by some oversensitive memoirist, or on a subjective reaction to someone's glance, or a casual remark. To prove the point, let us consider a social phenomenon that engaged masses of people in a sustained, risky, and undoubtedly spontaneous manifestation of their deeply held beliefs: workers' strikes.

In a very well researched study titled *Workers' Strikes in Poland in the Years 1945–1948* published in 1999[4]—that is, at a time when a diligent scholar had full access to all the pertinent source materials—a young historian, Łukasz Kamiński, meticulously recorded all the waves of workers' protests that swept through the country during those postwar years. And a lot was happening in Poland at the time. Communist authorities were successively emasculating autonomous social and political institutions, including labor unions and mass political parties with a long tradition—such as the Polish Socialist Party (PPS), then under the leadership of Zygmunt Żuławski, and the Polish Peasant Party (PSL), led at the time by Stanisław Mikołajczyk, Stanisław Mierzwa, and Stefan Korboński. By 1948 the *Gleichschaltung* of autonomous institutions in Poland was pretty much completed. They were either absorbed into Communist-sponsored organizations or banned, their leaders arrested, exiled, or silenced. And it turns out that during this entire period the working class put down its tools and went on strike *for reasons other than purely bread-and-butter issues* only once: in order to protest the publication in newspapers around the country of its own alleged denunciations of the pogrom in Kielce, where forty-two Jews had been killed by a Polish mob on July 4, 1946.[5]

This is difficult to understand at first, so let me simply quote from Kamiński's study:

On July 10 [1946] meetings were called in several Łódź factories in order to condemn the perpetrators of the Kielce pogrom. People were reluctant to sign condemnatory statements. Nevertheless such statements were published the next day in the newspapers. This resulted in protest strikes. The first ones to go on strike were workers from the Łódź Thread Factory, and from factories Scheibler and Grohman, who were joined by workers from Buhle, Zimmerman, Warta, Tempo Rasik, Hofrichter, Gampe and Albrecht, Gutman, Dietzel, Radziejewski, Wejrach, Kinderman, Wólczanka, and from two sawing workshops. At the beginning strikers demanded that false information be corrected [about factory workers' allegedly signing those protests]*; later a demand to release people condemned* [in the summary trial fourteen people were sentenced to death] *was added. Protesters were*

*very agitated; violence was used against those who
called for resuming work. . . . This kind of workers' reaction was not atypical for the rest of the
country. Crews in many factories refused to vote
resolutions condemning perpetrators of the pogrom.
In Lublin during a mass meeting of 1,500 rail-
waymen in this matter people were screaming,
"Down with the Jews," "Shame, they came to defend the Jews," "Bierut* [the President of Poland at the time] will not dare to sentence them
to death," "Wilno and Lwów have to be ours."*[6]*

There were many occasions during these
years to protest against the creeping communist takeover of Poland. But, obviously, this
was not the underlying motivation for the
wave of strikes following the Kielce pogrom.
And while these strikes make no sense as protest against some imaginary "Judeo-commune," they are perfectly understandable as a
sign of frustration that one could no longer
properly defend innocent Polish Christian
children threatened by the murderous designs
of the Jews. This was, literally, the gist of com-
plaints overheard by a Jewish woman injured
in the Cracow pogrom of August 1945, as she
was being taken to a hospital emergency room:

In the ambulance I heard comments of the escort-
ing soldier and the nurse who spoke about us as
Jewish scum, whom they have to save, and that
they shouldn't be doing this because we murdered
children, that all of us should be shot. We were
taken to the hospital of St. Lazarus at Kopernika
street. I was first taken to the operating room.
After the operation a solider appeared, who said
that he will take everybody to jail after the opera-
tions. He beat up one of the wounded Jews wait-
ing for an operation. He held us under a cocked
gun and did not allow us to take a drink of water.
A moment later two railroad-men appeared and
one said "it's a scandal that a Pole does not have
the civil courage to hit a defenseless person" and
he hit a wounded Jew. One of the hospital in-
mates hit me with a crutch. Women, including
nurses, stood behind the doors threatening us that
they are only waiting for the operation to be over
in order to rip us apart.[7]

In other words, postwar antisemitism was
widespread and predated any Communist at-
tempts to take power in Poland, because it was
firmly rooted in medieval prejudice about ritual murder. It was also embedded in the experience of war.

Why did the Wyrzykowski family have to flee from its farm? "Hershek, you're still alive?"—an incredulous sentence and a contemptuous look greeted Hershel Piekarz when he emerged from his hiding place in the woods.[8] Once again, such reactions were not derived from belief in some mythical "Judeo-commune" or anger over the Soviet-assisted Communist takeover of Poland abetted by the Jews. Hershel Piekarz, like other token Jews who survived the war, and the Wyrzykowski family, like other heroic Poles who had hidden Jews during the war at great peril and then, after the war, continued to hide this fact from their neighbors—all of them were not hated or feared as crypto-communists but rather as embarrassing witnesses to crimes that had been committed against the Jews. They could also point to the illicit material benefits that many continued to enjoy as a result of these crimes. Their existence was a reproach, calling forth pangs of conscience, as well as a potential threat.

C OLLABORATION

And what about a classic wartime theme that, as we know, has no place in Polish historiography of the period—collaboration?[1] After all, when Hitler launched his *Blitzkrieg* against the USSR in June 1941, German soldiers were received by the local population of former Polish territories (which were incorporated in 1939 into the Soviet Union) as an army of liberators! The commander of the underground Polish Home Army (AK), General Grot-Rowecki, sent a dispatch to London on July 8, 1941, informing the Polish government in exile about the friendly reception of the German army throughout the so-called *Kresy Wschodnie* (i.e., Eastern Borderlands).[2] "When the Germans attacked the Soviet army," writes a peasant from Białystok voivodeship, "the Polish population from these territories rather gladly received the Germans, not realizing that this was the most serious enemy of Polishness. In various little towns Germans were received with flowers, etc. . . . The sister of one of the inhabitants returned from Białystok at that time and told about the enthusiastic reception that the Germans received from the Polish population of the city." Or as in another characteristic recollection, also from the Białystok area: "People started talking about the pending war between Germans and Russkies, which people very much desired, hoping that the Germans would chase away the Russkies and we would remain in place and the Russians would not manage to deport all of us. . . . Finally in June 1941 a war broke out between Germans and Russkies, and a few days later Russians gave in. Great joy overcame people who were hiding from the Russkies as they were no longer afraid that they would be deported to Russia, and everybody who met a friend or a relative whom they had not seen for some time, their first words of greeting were: They will no longer deport us. It so happened that a priest from a neighboring parish was passing through our village the day after the Russkies moved out, and he called to everyone he saw: They won't deport us anymore. It is probable that Russians made a mistake by massively deporting Poles to Russia, and for this action local people really grew to hate the Russians."[3]

Indeed, over half of the prewar territory of the Polish state had been liberated by June and July of 1941 from Bolshevik rule, and the local population—with the exception of Jews, of course—recognized the event by welcoming the entering Wehrmacht units with open arms. Local residents promptly established administrative bodies compliant with German will and joined in the *Vernichtungskrieg* directed against the "Jews and the Commissars."[4] Ramotowski and his accomplices, after all, were put on trial because "they acted in a manner that fostered the interests of the German state," and so forth.

We come here upon a fascinating subject for a social psychologist—an overlay in collective memory of two episodes from this period. Two conquests of this territory, by the Red Army in 1939 and the Wehrmacht in 1941, seem grafted upon each other in preserved narratives. To put it simply, enthusiastic Jewish response to entering Red Army units was not a widespread phenomenon at all, and it is impossible to identify some innate, unique characteristics of Jewish collaboration with the Soviets during the period 1939–1941.[5] On the other hand, it is manifest that the local non-Jewish population enthusiastically greeted entering Wehrmacht units in 1941 and broadly engaged in collaboration with the Germans, up to and including participation in the exterminatory war against the Jews.

Thus it appears that the local non-Jewish population projected its own attitude toward the Germans in 1941 (this story remains a complete taboo and has never been studied in Polish historiography) onto an entrenched narrative about how the Jews allegedly behaved vis-à-vis the Soviets in 1939. The testimony by Finkelsztajn concerning how Radziłów's local Polish population received the Germans reads like a mirror image of widely circulating stories about Galician Jews receiving the Bolsheviks in 1939.

And what about the episode of the Soviets' recruiting secret police collaborators among

Polish underground activists, reported by Colonel Misiuriew and confirmed by the (auto)biography of Laudański? Could this be, perhaps, a particular instance of a more general phenomenon characteristic of this epoch? Aren't people compromised by collaboration with a repressive regime predestined, so to speak, to become collaborators of the next repressive regime that gains power over the same area? Such individuals would be inclined to demonstrate enthusiasm for new rulers and their policies right from the beginning, in order to accumulate sufficient credit in advance, to balance their liabilities in case their roles under a previous regime become known. Alternatively, they will collaborate because they are such an obvious and easy target for blackmail once their past record becomes known to new rulers. Nazism, let us repeat, following the German political philosopher Eric Voegelin, is a regime that taps into the evil instincts of human beings—not only because it elevates "rabble" into positions of power, but also because of "the simple man, who is a decent man as long as the society as a whole is in order but who then goes wild, without knowing what he is doing, when disorder arises somewhere and the society is no longer holding together."[6]

The Second World War, or, to be more precise, the Soviet and the German occupations that it brought, exposed provincial Poland for the first time to the modus operandi of totalitarian regimes. And it is not surprising that a society so afflicted did not stand up particularly well to the challenge, and that profound demoralization resulted from both collective experiences. To grasp this state of affairs, we need not even reach for subtle diagnosis by sophisticated intellectuals, such as the unsurpassed study of the impact of war on Polish society by literary scholar Kazimierz Wyka, for example.[7] It is enough to recall the plague of wartime banditry and alcoholism attested to by virtually any contemporaneous source; for illustration take a look, once again, at the collection of peasant memoirs about their wartime experiences that were submitted in 1948 to a public "contest" organized by the publishing house Czytelnik in Poland. Krystyna Kersten and Tomasz Szarota published submissions of some fifteen hundred authors in four thick volumes entitled *Polish Countryside, 1939–1948.*[8]

For me the most shattering exemplar of moral disintegration during those years, illustrating the breakdown of cultural taboos that prohibit the murder of innocent human beings, can be found in a story by a peasant woman from a hamlet near Wadowice—a story in which nobody gets killed, which must be read also as a hymn to love and selfless sacrifice. Karolcia Sapetowa, "a former maid," left this testimony with the staff of the Jewish Historical Commission, and it is now deposited at the Jewish Historical Institute in Warsaw:

Our family was composed of three children and their parents. The youngest, Sammy Hochheiser, a little girl, Sally, and the oldest one, Izzy. During the first year of the war the father was killed. When all the Jews were concentrated in the ghetto, we separated. Every day I went to the ghetto bringing along what I could, because I missed the children very much; I considered them as mine. When things were particularly bad in the ghetto, the children came over to my place and stayed with me until things quieted down.

*They felt at home at my place. In 1943 in March
the ghetto was liquidated. The youngest boy, by a
coincidence, was at my place on that day. I went
to the gate of the ghetto, which was surrounded
by SS men and Ukrainians* [auxiliary German
police formations made up of former citizens
of the USSR, sometimes referred to in short-
hand by Poles as "Ukrainians"] *on all sides.
People were running around like mad. Mothers
with children crowded helplessly near the gate.
Suddenly I saw the mother with Sally and Izzy.
The mother saw me as well, and she whispered
into the little girl's ear—"Go to Karolcia." Sally
without hesitation squeezed like a little mouse between the tall boots of the Ukrainians, who miraculously did not notice her. With her hands helplessly extended she ran toward me. Stiff with
fear I went with Sally and an aunt toward my
village, Witanowice, near Wadowice. The mother
and Izzy were resettled, and they have not been
heard from since. Life was very difficult, and
one must believe that only a miracle saved these
children.*

*At the beginning the children would go out of
the house, but when relationships got more tense,
I had to hide them inside. But even this did not*

help. Local people knew that I was hiding Jewish children, and threats and difficulties began from all directions—that the children should be handed over to the gestapo, that the whole village might be burned in reprisals, or murdered, etc. The village head was on my side, and this often gave me peace of mind. People who were more aggressive and insistent I appeased with an occasional gift, or paid them off.

But this did not last long. SS men were always looking around, and again protests started until a certain day they told me that we had to remove the children from this world, and they put together a plan to take the children to the barn and there, when they fell asleep, to chop their heads off with an ax.

I was walking around like mad. My elderly father completely stiffened. What to do? What am I to do? The poor miserable children knew about everything, and before going to sleep. they begged us: "Karolciu, don't kill us yet today. Not yet today." I felt that I was getting numb, and I decided that I would not give up the children at any price.

I got a brilliant idea. I put the children on a cart, and I told everybody that I was taking them out to drown them. I rode around the entire vil-

lage, and everybody saw me and they believed, and when the night came I returned with the children. . . .[9]

The story has a happy ending: the children survived, and Sapetowa declares with deep emotion that she will follow them anywhere because she loves them more than anything in the world. And we are left with a frightening realization that the population of a little village near Cracow sighed with relief only after its inhabitants were persuaded that one of their neighbors had murdered two small Jewish children.

How wartime demoralization played itself out among the Polish peasants, insofar as their attitude toward the Jews was concerned, has been described with unparalleled eloquence by one of the most important memoirists of this period, Dr. Zygmunt Klukowski, director of the county hospital in the village of Szczebrzeszyn, near Zamość. After all the Szczebrzeszyn Jews had been murdered, a process that Klukowski chronicled in devastating detail in his *Dziennik z lat okupacji zamojszczyzny* (Diary from the Years of Occupation of the Zamość Region), he writes, in despair, the following entry on November 26, 1942: "Peasants afraid of reprisals catch Jews in hamlets and bring them to town or sometimes kill them on the spot. In general some terrible demoralization has taken hold of people with respect to Jews. A psychosis took hold of them and they emulate the Germans in that they don't see a human being in Jews, only some pernicious animal, which has to be destroyed by all means, like dogs sick with rabies, or rats."[10]

And thus by partaking in the persecution of Jews during the summer of 1941, an inhabitant of these territories could simultaneously endear himself to the new rulers, derive material benefits from his actions (it stands to reason that active pogrom participants had first pick in the division of leftover Jewish property), and go along with local peasants' traditional animosity toward the Jews. If we add to this mix encouragement by the Nazis and an easily whipped-up sense that one was settling scores with the "Judeo-commune" for indignities suffered under the Soviet occupation—then who could resist such a potent, devilish mixture?[11] Of course, indispensable preconditions were prior brutalization of interpersonal relations, demoralization, and a general license to use violence. But these were exactly the methods employed and mechanisms put in place by both occupiers. It is not difficult to imagine that among the most active participants in the Jedwabne pogrom were several more secret collaborators of the NKVD (who were mentioned in a memorandum from Colonel Misiurew to Secretary Popov), in addition to Laudański, who conveniently told us in his autobiography that he had spied for the Soviets prior to killing the Jews for the Germans.

SOCIAL SUPPORT FOR STALINISM

But time did not come to a halt in 1941. And if we recognize that the mechanism I have just described is psychologically and sociologically plausible, then we are led to an interesting hypothesis about the coming to power and establishment of Communist rule in Poland in the years 1945–1948. In light of what has been said here so far, I would venture a proposition that in the process of Communist takeover in Poland after the war, the natural allies of the Communist Party, on the local level, were people who had been compromised during the German occupation.

We know, of course, that adherence to Communism was a very authentic commitment for a considerable number of people; and many supported the Communist Party before and after the war because they were true believers, and not because they were conformists, or because the Red Army was garrisoned across the country. But in addition to drawing from such a principled and idealistic pool of supporters, twentieth-century totalitarianisms always used manpower of a different sort. Among their most valuable operatives and confidants there were also people devoid of all principles. Many students of totalitarianism have made this point.[1]

Why wouldn't Voegelin's "rabble," which did the Nazis' dirty work in occupied Poland, reappear as the backbone of the Stalinist apparatus of power five years later? I have in mind the outer layer surrounding the core of stalwart Communists who, after all, were few and far between in Poland, as we know. In the name of what dearly held principles would they refuse to serve a new master? Why would they give up privileges that go with partaking in the local apparatus of power (read—of terror)? Why would they go to jail rather than to a police academy? Didn't Laudański have people of this ilk in mind when he wrote, "I believe that on shoulders like mine our workers' regime may rest"?

One may also reflect in this light about the process of the imposition of communist rule from the vantage point of society rather than that of the apparatus of power. From this point of view, I would propose that communities where Jews had been murdered by local inhabitants during the war were especially vulnerable to sovietization. If social atomization is a prerequisite for the effective establishment and consolidation of communist monopoly of power in society, then the only effective opposition against a communist takeover may come from social milieus that are capable of generating solidarity. The question, then, may be put in simple terms: Can a local community that has just been involved in the murder of its own neighbors generate such a response to a hostile takeover? How can anyone trust people who have murdered, or knowingly denounced to their murderers, other human beings? Furthermore, if we have acted as instruments of violence, in the name of what principles can we oppose the use of violence turned against us by somebody else?

The issue can best be taken up as a factual question, to be resolved by empirical research. But at this stage it suggests a very intriguing hypothesis, which inverts a well-established cliché about this period by positing that *antisemites rather than Jews were instrumental in establishing the Communist regime in Poland after the war*. After all, in numerous districts, counties, little towns, and cities of provincial Poland there were no more Jews after the war, because the few who survived fled as soon as they could.[2] But in the establishment of the "people's Poland" somebody had to take the business in hand throughout the country. So *kto kavo*, who was taking in hand whom, as Vladimir Ilich Lenin asked nearly a hundred years ago? If only because of the ideological evolution of the communist regime in Poland—which culminated in an outburst of official antisemitism in March 1968[3]—I would not outright dismiss a proposition that it was indigenous lumpenproletariat rather than Jews who served as the social backbone of Stalinism in Poland.

FOR A NEW HISTORIOGRAPHY

This so-called question of Polish-Jewish relations during the war is like a loose thread in the historiography of this period. If we grasp and pull it, the entire intricately woven tapestry comes undone. It seems to me that antisemitism polluted whole patches of twentieth-century Polish history and turned them into forbidden subjects, calling forth stylized interpretations whose role was to cover, like a fig leaf, what had really happened.

But the history of a society can be conceived as a collective biography. And just as in a biography—which is also composed of discrete episodes—everything in the history of a society is in rapport with everything else. And if at some point in this collective biography a big lie is situated, then everything that comes afterward will be devoid of authenticity and laced with fear of discovery. And instead of living their own lives, members of such a community will be suspiciously glancing over their shoulders, trying to guess what others think about what they are doing. They will keep diverting attention from shameful episodes buried in the past and go on "defending Poland's good name," no matter what. They will take all setbacks and difficulties to be a consequence of deliberate enemy conspiracies. Poland is not an exception in this respect among European countries. And like several other nations, in order to reclaim its own past, Poland will have to tell its past to itself anew.

An appropriate memento is to be found—where else?—in Jedwabne. Inscriptions were engraved there on two stone monuments commemorating the time of war. One of them simply propagates a lie by stating that 1,600 Jedwabne Jews were killed by the Nazis. The other, which was erected in post-1989 Poland, is more revealing. It reads, "To the memory of about 180 people including 2 priests who were murdered in the territory of Jedwabne district in the years 1939–1956 by the NKWD, the Nazis, and the secret police [UB]." Signed, "society [*społeczeństwo*]". And thus it either suggests that there were no Jews in Jedwabne at all, or else offers an unwitting admission of the crime. For, indeed, the 1,600 Jedwabne Jews were killed neither by the NKVD, nor by the Nazis, nor by the Stalinist secret police. Instead, as we now know beyond reasonable doubt, and as Jedwabne citizens knew all along, it was their neighbors who killed them.

P OSTSCRIPT

The Jedwabne issue broke into the mass media in Poland with the broadcasting of Agnieszka Arnold's documentary *Where Is My Older Brother Cain?*, including a brief segment of conversation with Śleszyński's daughter in April 2000, and brilliant investigative reporting by Andrzej Kaczyński for the daily newspaper *Rzeczpospolita* in May. His first article, "Całopalenie," devoted exclusively to the Jedwabne massacre of Jews, was published on the front page of this respected daily with nationwide circulation of several hundred thousand copies on May 5, 2000. The follow-up article appeared two weeks later, on May 19. On the same day the Polish-language edition of *Neighbors* was launched at Warsaw's International Book Fair.

As Kaczyński's reporting confirmed, Jedwabne residents knew well that Jedwabne Jews had been murdered by their neighbors during the war. This was, and remains, an uncontested issue. Furthermore, in conversations held in the ensuing weeks among Jedwabne's mayor, the town's citizens, and Catholic Church representatives both in Jedwabne and in Łomża, as well as representatives of the Jewish community from Warsaw who came to Jedwabne, a consensus began to emerge that the burial site of the Jewish victims will have to be properly identified and marked as a cemetery, that the monument and inscription on it will have to be changed to reflect the truth of the events, and that the whole story will have to be investigated and told in all its details. Indeed in August 2000 the newly established Institute of National Memory, which has the authority to issue indictments in cases of "crimes against the Polish nation," announced that it would open an investigation of the Jedwabne massacre, and that any perpetrators found still alive and liable to prosecution would be brought to trial. In conclusion, I believe that we have reached a threshhold at which the new generation, raised in Poland with freedom of speech and political liberties, is ready to confront the unvarnished history of Polish-Jewish relations during the war.

FRIENDS

Photograph taken immediately after the war.
Seated from the left: Antonina (Antosia) Wyrzy-
kowska, Szmul Wasersztajn, and Leja Kubrzańska
(Kubran). Janek Kubrzański is standing behind
Wyrzykowska. Leja and Janek Kubrzański and
Szmul Wasersztajn, together with four other Jews,
were saved by the Wyrzykowski family, who hid
them throughout the occupation on their farm in
Janczewo, near Jedwabne.

A well-known shoemaker in Jedwabne, Josek
Kubrzański— father of Janek Kubrzański (Jack
Kubran)—with a friend.

Malka Zieleniec, Rywka Luber (left for Palestine), and Sorka Berlin. Janek Kubrzański
(Jack Kubran) is standing behind on the left.

Ovadia, Miriam, and Szlomo Bursztajn.

Lejb Bromsztajn in Polish army uniform, with
two friends.

Three Piekarz (Baker) brothers, with their mother.

The Piekarz family.

Millers from Jedwabne,
Eli and Moshe-David
Pecynowicz, and Yenta
Pecynowicz, Eli's wife—
uncles and aunt of the
Piekarz brothers and of
Nieł2wicki.

Parents of Wiktor Niełáwicki (Avigdor
Kochav). His mother's maiden name was
Stern; hence he changed his name in Israel
to Kochav, which means "star" in Hebrew.

Judke Nadolnik, one of the three kheyder
teachers (melamed) in Jedwabne with his
family. One of the older daughters left for
Palestine. The youngest, Gitele, was killed in
the square in Jedwabne on July 10, 1941, by
having her head cut off.

Daughters of Moshe Ibram, who was a wealthy
store owner in Jedwabne. Circumstances of the
murder of Judes Ibram are mentioned by one
of the witnesses in Ramotowski's trial.

Rywka Hurwicz, owner of a store in Jedwabne,
with her children. Her son, Moshe, left for
Palestine.

Malka Hurwicz, with her husband and child.

The Atłasowicz family.

The family of Abraham Szlepak, who was a
shochet (ritual slaughterer) in Jedwabne. He
was married to Frumka Pecynowicz, related
to the Piekarz family, with whom he had
nine children.

Two daughters of a butcher from Jedwabne,
Itzhak Atlas.

The family Bromsztajn. The elder Bromsztajn
was a house painter and a learned man. He was
a leading personality in one of Jedwabne's
shtibls (study houses), called Hevra Bakhurim.
Lejb Bromsztajn appears in another photograph in a Polish army uniform.

Another kheyder teacher from Jedwabne, Itzhak Adamski, with his family. One of the daughters left for Palestine.

Judka Ebersztajn-Piekarz, with his family.

Jaakov Sender Turberg with his wife, Sarah.

Hanah Danowska, daughter of one of three
kheyder teachers (melamed) in Jedwabne,
together with her husband, Garbarski, from
Łomża and daughter Joshpa.

ORGANIZATIONS

Children from a Jewish class in Jedwabne's
public school with their teachers—Szeme-
równa and Podróżnik.

Halutz organization in Jedwabne in 1922.

Yedwabne, 1930 P.I.T.H.

Zionist organization in Jedwabne in 1930.

Halutz organization in Jedwabne in 1930.

DOCUMENTS AND MAPS

A sample of court documents, investigation
protocols, and clemency petitions produced by
perpetrators of the Jedwabne massacre that
formed the principal source for this book.

PROTOKÓŁ

przesłuchania podejrzanego

665 670

Łomża dnia 16 stycznia 1949 r.

Bezpieczeństwa Publicznego w

przesłuchał w charakterze podejrzanego

Nazwisko i imię

Imiona rodziców

Data i miejsce urodzenia

Miejsce zamieszkania majątek

Narodowość pol

Wyznanie

Zawód

Przynależność do R.K.U. Ostrów

Stosunek do służby wojskowej

Stan rodzinny

Stan majątkowy

Odznaczenia i ordery

Karalność

Nr. akt. Okr. 33/49 80ć 123

Protokół rozprawy głównej.

200 201

Sąd Okręgowy w Łomży Dnia 15 maja 1949 r.

Sprawa Bolesława Ramotowskiego i 21 innych

oskarżonego z art. 1 p 2 dekr. z dn. 31 VIII 1944 r.

Obecni:

Przewodniczący i referent Sędzia S.O. Małecki

Ławnicy Władysław Skarżewa

Stanisław Stępkowski

Prokurator B. Januszek

Protokólant B. Skoszkowska

POW. URZ. BEZP. PUBL. ściśle tajne

W ŁOMŻY

REFERAT I—szy Łomża, dnia 24.I.1949r.

L. dz. .... AG.1/49 do

ZATRZYMANY .... NACZELNIKA WYDZIAŁU I-go

Dnia ....1949r. WOJ.URZ.BEZP.PUBL.

w BIAŁYMSTOKU

R A P O R T Za zgodność

likwidacyjny.

W ślad za raportem z dn.22.I.49r.za Nr.L.dz. 123 AG.1/49

zgłaszam:

I. PRZEBIEG AKCJI LIKWIDACJI

Dnia 9.I.49r. wyjechał maszyną ob-wą Jedwabne i aresztować:

1) RAMOTOWSKIEGO Bolesława s. Pawła i Józefy, ur.1.IV.1911r.
w Jantrowie,zam.Jedwabne ul. Łomżyńska,s.polak,rzym.kat.wykszt.
1 oddział szkoły powszechnej,

2) ZEJER Stanisław s. Teofila i Józefy,ur.24.X.1898r. Okilkowie
zam.Jedwabne,pow.łomża,polak,rzym.kat., rolnik,wykształc.oddz.
szkoły powszechnej, bezpartyjny,

3) LIPIŃSKI Czesław s. .... Juna i Leokadii,ur.16.X.1920r.w Grzymałach
polak,rzym.kat., pałnik, zam.Jedwabne,pow.łomża,wykszt.5 oddz.
szkoły powsz., kawalar, bezpartyjny,

4) JANOWSKI Aleksander s. Stanisława i Józefy,ł.V.1909r. wieś
Grzymki,pietrasze,zap.Jedwabne,pow.łomża,polak,rzym.kat.,rybanik,
wykszt. 5 oddz.szkoły pow., żonaty, bezpartyjny.

5) DĄBROWSKI Władysław s. Józefa i Katarzyny,ur.25.V.1890r.
w Jedwabne,zam.Jedwabne,pów.łomża,polak,rzym.kat.,
bezpartyjny.

6) TARNACKI Feliks s. Juna i Konstancji,ur.16.V.1907r.w Jedwabne,
zam. Jedwabne,sł.Kościuszki,pow.łomża,polak,rzym.kat.,
wozicel,bezpartyjny.

7) CHRZANOWSKI Józef s. Kasparego .... i Łucyja .... ,ur.1.XI.1880r.
w Kuchach,zam.Jedwabne,pow.łomża,polak,rzym.kat.,stolarz,
stan majatkowy 8 ha ziemi,żonaty,bezpartyjny,analfabet,

8) GÓRSKI Romuald Ludwika i Wiktorii,ur.16.VIII.1904r.w Konopkach,
zam.Jedwabne,pow.łomża,polak,rzym.kat.wykszt.5 oddz.szkoły pow.
stan majątkowy 3 ha ziemi,żonaty,bezpartyjny.

9) NIEBRZYDOWSKI Antoni s. Andrzeja i Józefy,ur.l.V.1901r.wieś
Burzec,zam.Jedwabne,pow.łomża,polak,rzym.kat.,plugarz,,wykszt.
1 oddział szkoły pow.,żonaty,bezpartyjny.

10) MICIURA Władysław s. Juna i Józefy,ur.21.IX.1901r.w Jedwabnym
zam. Jedwabne,pow.łomża,polak,rzym.kat.,zajęcie stolarz,wykszt.
1 oddz.szkoły pow.,żonaty,bezpartyjny.

11) ŻYLUK Marcin .... Ludwika i Katarzyny,ur.25.IV.1919r.wieś Folwark,
zam.Jedwabne,pow.łomża,polak,rzym.kat.,robotnik,wykszt.1 oddz.
szkoły pow.żonaty,bezpartyjny.

12) ŻYLUK Józef s. Ludwika i Katarzyny,ur.12.I.1910r. w Baczkowie,
zam. Jedwabne,pow.łomża,polak,rzym.kat.,robotnik,analfabeta,
żonaty,bezpartyjny.

Poland under Soviet and German occupation,
1939–1941.

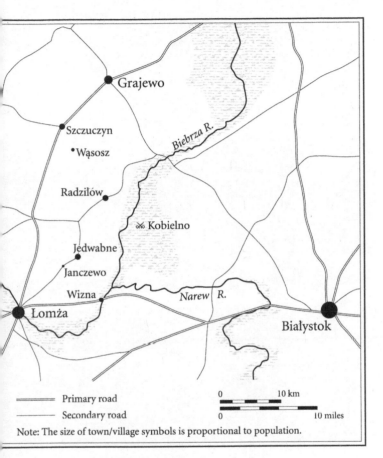

"Bermuda Triangle" of July 1941 massacres
of Jews by their neighbors.

NOTES

INTRODUCTION

1. The phrase is the coinage of Paulina Preis in her book *Biurokracja totalna* (Paris: Instytut Literacki, 1969). For a general discussion of totalitarianism as a "spoiler state," see the concluding chapter of my *Revolution from Abroad: Soviet Conquest of Poland's Western Ukraine and Western Belorussia* (Princeton: Princeton University Press, 1988).

2. Hannah Arendt, "Organized Guilt and Universal Responsibility," in *Essays in Understanding, 1930–1954* (New York: Harcourt, Brace, and Co., 1994), p. 126.

3. The term makes its initial appearance in a statement published following the Hitler-Pétain meeting at Montoire, on October 24, 1940: "*Une collaboration a été envisagée entre nos deux pays*," the aged marshal said in a radio appeal to his compatriots; "*J'en ai accepté le principe*" (Gerhard Hirschfeld, "Collaboration in Nazi Occupied France: Some Introductory Remarks," in *Collaboration in France: Politics and Culture during the Nazi Occupation, 1940–1944,*

ed. G. Hirschfeld and P. Marsh [Oxford: Berg, 1989], p. 2). And we have it on the authority of lexicographers that such a narrow meaning (limited to the circumstances of German occupations during World War II) constitutes virtually all that the concept denotes in various languages. The last prewar edition (1933) of the *Oxford English Dictionary* does not offer a definition for the word *collaboration* in the sense that interests us here. *Collaboration* is generally defined there (2:613 in the 1961 reprint) as "work in conjunction with another or others, esp. in a literary or artistic production, or the like." Robert's dictionary of 1953 gives the following explication for a special meaning of collaboration (which otherwise pertains in French also to common pursuits in artistic matters): "Mouvement des Français qui durant occupation Allemande (1940–1944) désiraient travailler au redressement de la France en cooperation avec l'Allemagne" (p. 819). Bataglia, in his dictionary of the Italian language from 1964, as the fourth meaning of collaboration (3:279) refers to involvement with occupation authorities, and specifically the German ones during World War II ("per lo più con riferimento al periodo d'occupazione tedesca durante la Seconda Guerra Mondiale)." *Encyclopedia Brockhaus* of 1970 (10:350) defines the term primarily by reference to the actions of Pétain's government in France; though in small print it also informs the reader that the word may be used more generally.

4. See my "Themes for a Social History of War Experience and Collaboration," in *The Politics of Retribution in Europe: World War II and Its Aftermath*, ed. Istvan Deák, Jan T. Gross, and Tony Judt (Princeton: Princeton University Press, 2000), pp. 23–32.

5. Istvan Deák, "Introduction," in Deák, Gross, and Judt, *The Politics of Retribution in Europe*, p. 4.

6. Heda Margolius Kovaly, *Under a Cruel Star: A Life in Prague, 1941–1968* (New York: Holmes and Meier, 1997), p. 45.

7. For a general discussion of these and related issues, see my *Polish Society under German Occupation—Generalgouvernement, 1939–1944* (Princeton: Princeton University Press, 1979).

8. Norman Davies, *God's Playground: A History of Poland* (New York: Columbia University Press, 1982).

9. In a previous study I have questioned reigning stereotypes on this subject in Polish historiography—see *Upiorna dekada. Trzy eseje o stereotypach na temat Żydów, Polaków, Niemców, i komunistów* (Cracow: Universitas, 1998). An abridged version of this book has appeared in English as "A Tangled Web: Confronting Stereotypes concerning the Relations between Poles, Germans, Jews, and Communists," in Deák, Gross, and Judt, *The Politics of Retribution in Europe*, pp. 74–129. Here I will, therefore, merely signal a few points to orient the reader as to how the subsequent narrative is framed in response to queries arising from the standpoint of such conventional views.

10. *Szmalcownik* is a word of unequivocal opprobrium in the Polish language. It refers specifically to individuals who made a profession in German-occupied Poland during the Second World War of blackmailing Jews who were trying to "pass" on the Aryan side—a crime punishable by a death sentence from the occupation authorities. The word itself derives from *szmalec*, literally lard, but in colloquial usage meaning also cash, loot.

11. I provide a critical analysis of prevailing views on the subject in *Upiorna dekada*.

12. I refer here to Raul Hilberg's *Perpetrators, Victims, Bystanders: The Jewish Catastrophe, 1933–1945* (New York: Aaron Asher Books, 1992). Of course, the distinction

has implicitly been present in Holocaust studies for a long time. Hilberg, however, very deliberately calls our attention to the situational context in which the Shoah was perpetrated. The quotation is from a very useful introduction by Omer Bartov to the volume he recently edited for the Rewriting Histories series: *The Holocaust: Origins, Implementation, Aftermath* (London: Routledge, 2000), p. 8.

OUTLINE OF THE STORY

1. The report, dated January 24, 1949, is currently held together with other control-investigative files of the Łomża Public Security Office (*Urząd Bezpieczeństwa Publicznego w Łomży*) in the archives of the Office for State Security in Białystok (*Wydział Ewidencji i Archiwum Delegatury Urzędu Ochrony Państwa*, later referenced as UOP). We also learn from it that in addition to the fifteen arrested in Jedwabne "seven people were not apprehended, because they are hiding in unknown localities."

2. I borrow this expression from a pathbreaking study by Christopher Browning, entitled *Ordinary Men: Reserve Battalion 101 and the Final Solution in Poland* (New York: Harper and Collins, 1992).

3. A mimeographed publication *Głos Jedwabnego*, in its June 1986 issue, informs us that in 1949, the city "together with Kajetanowo, Kossaki, and Biczki suburbs comprised 2,150 inhabitants."

4. I quote in this study from the files of two court cases, which are kept in the archive of the Main Commission for Investigation of Crimes against the Polish Nation (hereafter MC)—*Główna Komisja Badania Zbrodni Przeciwko Narodowi Polskiemu*—transferred in the year 2000 into the newly established Institute of National Memory—*Instytut Pamięci Narodowej*. The case against Bolesław Ramotowski and others is filed under catalog number SOŁ 123; the case

against Józef Sobuta, tried in 1953 and also pertaining to the cirumstances of the massacre of the Jedwabne Jews, is filed under catalog number SWB 145. In those files consecutive sheets, rather than pages (recto and verso), are numbered by hand. The sentence quoted can be found in MC, SOŁ 123, on p. 3 (I will hereafter use the notation form 123/3).

I would like to thank Professor Andrzej Paczkowski for facilitating my access to the archives of the Main Commission at the time when they were being packed prior to their imminent transfer into the custody of the recently established (1999) Institute of National Memory. I also want to thank him and his collaborators from the Laboratory of Late Modern [*Najnowszej*] Polish History at the Institute of Political Studies of the Polish Academy of Sciences in Warsaw (ISP PAN), for the opportunity to present and discuss initial findings of my research.

5. In a document entitled "Report concerning the Beginning of Investigation of the Case" (*Meldunek o wszczęciu rozpracowania sprawy*) we find the following information filed under the rubric "History of How the Investigation Was Initiated" (*historia wszczęcia rozpracowania*): "A letter was sent to the Ministry of Justice by a Jewess Calka Migdał, who escaped when the jews were being murdered in Jedwabne, and who saw everything and also who took part in the murder of jews in 1941 in Jedwabne." But her letter is not included in the files, and we do not know when was it sent to the Ministry of Justice. One more document is held in the files that alerted the Security Office to wartime crimes in Jedwabne, this one dated December 30, 1947. Entitled "Report," it reads as follows: "I hereby report that in the town of Jedwabne in the Łomża County there lived during the German occupation and worked in the municipality as a mayor citizen Karolak Marian. His

description: heavyset, round face, hair used to be dark now mostly gray, about six feet tall, clear face without any characteristic marks. Still under the Germans he was arrested by the German authorities, as far as I know because of all the riches he took from the jews and did not divide equally with the germans. He was released and then once again taken by the germans, and he disappeared. Recently, on December 1, 1947, I was in Warsaw in the Grochowska district and I saw personally how the same Karolak Marian walked in the street. As soon as he saw me, he disappeared. I wanted to report him to the militia or some other authorities, but no one was in the street at the time . . ." (UOP). The Security Office was not able to find and arrest Karolak in subsequent years.

6. Jewish Historical Institute (JHI) in Warsaw, collection no. 301, document no. 152 (301/152). Throughout my translations I try to preserve the linguistic and orthographic awkwardness of the original documents being quoted. Collection no. 301 at the Institute, called "Individual Depositions," contains over seven thousand depositions collected immediately after the war from survivors of the Holocaust by a then established Jewish Historical Commission. These are probably the most important, because quasi-contemporaneous, sources for the study of the Holocaust period in Poland. The Jewish Historical Commission had branches in several larger towns (capitals of Poland's voivodeships, i.e., largest territorial units of administration) where Jews resided at the time. Thus, for example, Wasersztajn's deposition was made before the Jewish Historical Commission in Białystok, on April 5, 1945. At the bottom of the page we find an additional note: "Witness Szmul Wasersztajn, written down by E. Sztejman; chairman of the Voivodeship Jewish Historical Commission, M. Turek; freely translated from the Yiddish language by M. Kwater."

We should take note, as well, that various people left several depositions about their experiences, and they may vary somewhat as to details. For example, a second Wasersztajn's deposition, filed at JHI under 301/613, states that fifty young Jews were murdered at the cemetery, and that altogether eighteen Jews from Jedwabne survived the war.

7. The film was aired on the main channel of Polish state television in April 2000 and was very well received by critics. The Jedwabne episode occupies but two minutes in a sixty-three-minute-long documentary feature. I want to thank Agnieszka Arnold for making available to me the script of her interviews conducted in Jedwabne, as well as for her not objecting to my using the title *Neighbors* for this book, a title she had planned all along to use for her documentary film about the Jedwabne massacre.

SOURCES
1. Such reports, entitled *Ereignismeldung UdSSR*, were distributed by the RSHA (Reich's Main Security Office) daily from June 22, 1941. They can be found in the Bundesarchiv in Koblenz under R 58/214. Excerpts from these situational reports were published in English as *The Einsatzgruppen Reports*, ed. Yitzhak Arad, Shmuel Krakowski, and Shmuel Spector, (New York: The Holocaust Library, 1989). Neither David Engel nor Christopher Browning, who both thoroughly know German archives pertaining to the period, was familiar with the name of the town Jedwabne.

2. Wiktor Nielawicki (after the war he settled in Israel and changed his name to Avigdor Kochav) survived the pogrom and later, pretending to be of Polish ethnic background, joined an anti-Nazi guerrilla detachment. He returned to Białystok voivodeship with two colleagues from his outfit sometime in 1944. One day they came upon a

signpost for Jedwabne, and his companion recalled the name from a German documentary newsreel he had seen in Warsaw in 1941. It showed, he remembered, how Poles had murdered the local Jews after the Germans arrived there in the opening days of their offensive against the USSR (conversation with Niełnawicki, February 2000). Also, in the files of Ramotowski's case we find the following sentence in the deposition of Julia Sokołowska (whom I will later quote more extensively): "Germans stood to the side and took pictures and later showed the population how Poles murdered the Jews" (MC, SOŁ 123/630). In the context of Niełnawicki's statement I think she must have meant that the Germans had later shown the film of the pogrom in town, rather than, for example, organized a photographic exhibit.

3. Several former Jewish inhabitants of Jedwabne were alive during the time I was writing this book, and I talked with them about prewar Jewish life in town, as well as about the circumstances of the July 1941 mass murder. They are Rabbi Jacob Baker (Piekarz), who left Jedwabne in 1938, and thanks to whose efforts the memorial book of Jedwabne Jews has been published; his brother Hershel Baker, who survived the war by hiding in the vicinity of Jedwabne; Avigdor Kochav (Wiktor Niełnawicki) from Wizna, who was in Jedwabne on July 10, 1941; Mietek Olszewicz, who likewise survived the pogrom in Jedwabne and was one of the seven Jews later hidden by the Wyrzykowski family; his, at the time, fiancée, Ela Sosnowska, and Leja Kubrańska (Kubran), who were also hidden by the Wyrzykowskis; and Szmul Wasersztajn (who died on February 9, 2000). I also spoke with Mrs. Antonina (Antosia, as her wards lovingly call her) Wyrzykowska; Mr. Jan Cytrynowicz from Łomża, whose family converted to Catholicism before the war in Wizna; and Mrs. Adamczyk from

Jedwabne. Various older inhabitants of the town, whom I approached during my visit to Jedwabne, either did not remember much or happened to have been away from Jedwabne on the day of the massacre.

4. The Ringelblum Archive, currently held at the Jewish Historical Institute in Warsaw, is a set of documents discovered under the rubble of the Warsaw ghetto at 68 Nowolipki Street. In September 1946, ten metal containers holding the first part of the collection were excavated based on a tip offered by Hersz Wasser, one of the members of the team who assembled this collection. Four years later, in December 1950, during the repair work on the same building, the second part of the collection was discovered hidden in two large metal milk cans. The third part, buried at 34 Świętojerska Street, was lost and will probably never be recovered.

The Ringelblum Archive consists of nearly six thousand documents (some in two or three copies), mainly in the Polish, Yiddish, and German languages. They are a legacy left by an underground institution known as the Ghetto Archive (and also by the secret name *Oneg Shabbat*) and were compiled from the autumn of 1940 to the summer of 1942.

Emanuel Ringelblum, born in November 1900 and killed by the Nazis in March 1944, was a historian, teacher, and social and political activist. The *Oneg Shabbat* group, which he organized and whose work he coordinated, was not only a documentation center; it also distributed surveys and collected information through the application of modern social research methods. It aimed at establishing comprehensive documentation concerning the overall situation and the process of destruction of the Jewish community in Poland in the years of the Second World War.

5. In the Ramotowski trial the following sentences were pronounced: Józef Chrzanowski, Marian Żyluk, Czesław Laudański, Wincenty Gościcki, Roman Zawadzki, Aleksander Łojewski, Eugeniusz Śliwecki, and Stanisław Sielawa were acquitted; Karol Bardoń was sentenced to death; Jerzy Laudański to fifteen years; Zygmunt Laudański, Władysław Miciura, and Bolesław Ramotowski to twelve years; Stanisław Zejer and Czesław Lipiński to ten years; Józef Żyluk, Antoni Niebrzydowski, Władysław Dąbrowski, Feliks Tarnacki, and Roman Górski to eight years.

Archival documents contain some baffling discrepancies concerning which individuals were put on trial in this case. In the court files of the case against Ramotowski we find a handwritten "Protocol of the Main Trial" (*Protokół rozprawy głównej*), neatly prepared by a court stenographer, Cz. Mroczkowska, on May 16, 1949, and we read in it the following sentence: "All the accused are present at the trial." There follows a list of twenty-two names accompanied by biographical data on each of the accused (MC, SOŁ 123/200–202). In the control-investigative files of the Łomża Security Office, on the other hand, we find a "Report on the Conduct and Result of the Court Case" (*Raport o przebiegu i wyniku rozprawy sądowej*) filed on the next day, May 17, 1949, which was forwarded to the superior Białystok Voievodship Security Office from Łomża (UOP). This report enumerates but sixteen names of the accused; moreover, its list includes a certain Aleksander Janowski, who appears in the trial merely as a witness (he had originally been arrested on January 8, 1949, but was subsequently released from preventive detention). In the most important respect, however, the two documents overlap—they give identical information as to who was found guilty and what sentences they received.

I am at a loss to explain the discrepancies. It seems to me that a court document, filed publicly, is more reliable than a secret police report in this respect. In the end, this may be just one more indication that the trial of the Jedwabne accused was a routine, slapdash job for the security police, who were therefore not overly attentive to details.

The case against Józef Sobuta also deserves a brief commentary. He was already under investigation when Ramotowski's case was brought before the judicial authorities, but did not appear among the accused because he was in a psychiatric ward at the time. The Łomża Security Office (*Urząd Bezpieczeństwa*, UB) clearly did not want to delay the opening of the trial and informed the prosecutor's office on March 24, 1949, that Sobuta would be arrested upon his release from the hospital.

It is quite likely that Sobuta was faking mental illness. After leaving the hospital, he was not arrested but, instead, took residence in the city of Łódź, where he ran a shop until he was sentenced to twelve months of corrective labor for attempting to bribe a state functionary. Two psychiatrists evaluated his mental competence to stand trial in 1953. During the medical examination Sobuta could not tell what charges had been filed against him. Asked when he had left the labor camp, he answered, "When the gate was opened," and generally gave the impression of being mentally impaired. But the doctors pronounced him competent to stand trial (MC, SWB 145/205). During his investigation, as a rule, he asserted that he remembered nothing. But with respect to one issue that could have put him in serious trouble—as many witnesses pointed out, he was the main instigator of the dismantling of the Lenin monument in Jedwabne during the pogrom—he told a very clever little fib (MC, SWP 145/267–270). On the basis of several depositions, both in his trial and in the 1949 trial of

Ramotowski, I am convinced that he was one of the most active participants of the pogrom. Why was he acquitted, then?

He was served with a dual indictment in 1953. Sobuta was accused of "taking part in burning alive hundreds of Jews in the village of Jedwabne, and by doing so of having been of assistance to the hitlerite authorities of the german state from June 22, 1941, to June 1944; and also of having identified for the german gendarmerie a functionary of the militia and a member of the Communist Party, Czesław Krupiński, or Kupiecki, who was then murdered by the gendarmes" (MC, SWB 145/199). And when the investigating officer in Białystok, a certain Wiktor Chomczyk, came to the conclusion on October 2, 1953, that there were no grounds for prosecution of Sobuta "in the matter of accusation concerning identifying for the germans Czesław Kupiecki, a former militiamen during the Soviet administration [from September 1939 to June 1941 Jedwabne was in the part of Poland occupied by the Soviet Union]"—the whole case promptly lost momentum, and Sobuta was soon acquitted (MC, SWB 145/274). Clearly "taking part in burning alive hundreds of Jews" during the occupation was not an offense that would warrant stern prosecution by a Stalinist judiciary without some aggravating circumstances.

6. Why is it that defendants spilled the beans, so to speak, instead of incriminating the Germans, for instance? In the first place, one is always caught by surprise and fearful when questioned by the police. Moreover, in this case the accused did not have much room to maneuver, because the massacre had been an open and public event, and everybody knew what had happened. They could not brazenly lie to UB interrogators, who also knew what had happened and would certainly have given them a brutal beating if they

had tried to be insolent. So, naturally, they tried to play down their own involvement. But the general outlines of the event could not be denied or grossly misrepresented.

7. MC, SOŁ 123/2.

8. MC, SOŁ 123/296.

9. I have in mind not only the Kremlin's so-called Doctors' Plot, or the antisemitic context of the Slánský trial in Czechoslovakia, but a general ideological trend that by then was emanating from Moscow. Nicolas Werth writes about this in his brilliant series of essays published in *Stalinisme et nazisme, histoire et memoire comparées*. "During the 1939–1949 decade, while territorial expansion, war, and sovietization of occupied territories was taking place, altogether some 3,200,000 people had been subjected to deportation. The vast majority of the deportees were selected on the basis of ethnic criteria, and not on class-based criteria as was the case during 'de-kulakization.' " A significant proportion of the deportees during these years, I may add, were ethnic Poles. "The enemy, clearly, changed its appearance in the context of the second [i.e., postwar] Stalinism. This period was characterized by anachronistic, regressive obscurantism, such as antisemitism, for instance (utterly absent among the first generation of Bolshevik leaders), and xenophobia articulated in many different manners in the form of praise for the 'Great Motherland Russia.' The principal enemy of Communism from this time on was defined through the use of ethnic categories" (Nicolas Werth, "Logiques de violence dans l'URSS stalinienne, " in *Stalinisme et nazisme, histoire et memoire comparées*, ed. Henry Rousso, [Brussels: Editions Complexe, 1999], pp. 122, 123).

10. Particularly interesting in this respect are appeals for clemency and parole. Such requests were so numerous in this case that the Łomża District Court wrote

on April 2, 1954, to the Voivodeship Court in Białystok requesting custody of the files: "Because eleven people in the case are sentenced to long prison terms, the local prosecutor's office is in charge of supervising the carrying out of the penalty, and prisoners are constantly filing for clemency, parole, etc." (MC, SWB 145/786).

BEFORE THE WAR

1. *Łomża*, topographical map of Poland no. N-34–105/106 (Warsaw: Wojskowe Zakłady Kartograficzne, 1997), verso.

2. Kazimierz and Maria Piechotkowie, *Bramy nieba: bóżnice drewniane na ziemiach dawnej Rzeczypospolitej* (Warsaw: Krupski i S-ka, 1996), pp. 231–232. Information concerning the history of Jedwabne as well as the prewar life of the Jewish community is provided on the basis of two sources. One of them is *Yedwabne: History and Memorial Book* ed. Julius L. Baker and Jacob L. Baker (Jerusalem and New York: The Yedwabner Societies in Israel and the United States of America, 1980) (hereafter *Yedwabne*). I am also using an untitled typescript by Henryk Majecki, former director of state archives in Białystok, a historian and author of many works about the history of the Białystok region. As Majecki informs us, "there are only a few sources concerning the interwar history of Jedwabne. Documents from the city hall and the *gmina* office have not been preserved, nor were files of various social institutions or local schools. There are no memoirs about Jedwabne from this period or county archives for the Kolno and Łomża Counties of which, successively, Jedwabne was a part" (Majecki, typescript, p. 41).

3. *Yedwabne*, p. 8.

4. Ibid., p. 20. An elderly Polish pharmacist, who was still living in the village in 1998, recalled that among

Jedwabne Jews "there weren't any so-called intelligentsia. All were craftsmen, and workers of a simple kind, coachmen" (transcript of interviews for the film *Where Is My Older Brother Cain?* [*Gdzie jest mój brat Kain?*, unpublished script], p. 489).

5. "Franek and Stashek" he called the Sielawa brothers, using diminutives during our conversation in New York. Both of them are mentioned by Wasersztajn among the worst murderers. Stanisław Sielawa was among the accused during Ramotowski's trial. The episode concerning potato peels delivered by the little Sielawa sister is described in *Yedwabne*, pp. 55, 56.

6. *Where Is My Older Brother Cain?*, p. 489.

7. Numerically the largest political party in interwar Poland, with a strong antisemitic component in its political program.

8. Gershon David Hundert has written a very interesting study of the eighteenth-century Jewish community in Opatów (Opt), in which he provides specific information about such "gifts" paid by the community from 1728 to 1784: *The Jews in a Private Polish Town: The Case of Opatów in the Eighteenth Century* (Baltimore: Johns Hopkins University Press, 1992), pp. 98–104.

9. The Catholic clergy in Łomża and vicinity were politically sympathetic to the National Democratic party. Tadeusz Frączek writes in his recently completed doctoral dissertation ("Formacje zbrojne obozu narodowego na Białostocczyźnie w latach 1939–1956," Wojskowy Instytut Historyczny [Military Historical Institute], Warsaw, file no. 76) how the bishop of Łomża, Stanisław Łukomski, wrote pastoral letters in April of 1928, just before an important election, telling his parishioners "not to vote for the socialists, the communists, or the sympathizers of so-called peasant parties." After the elections he forbade Easter proces-

sions in those parishes where votes had been cast in support of peasant parties (pp. 36–37).

SOVIET OCCUPATION, 1939–1941

1. *Documents on German Foreign Policy*, ed. R. J. Sontag (Washington, D.C.: U.S. Government Printing Office, 1954), 7:247.

2. Several hundred thousand Polish citizens had been deported into the Soviet interior during the twenty-month-long Soviet rule over the half of Poland occupied by the Red Army in September 1939. Then, in the aftermath of Hitler's attack on the USSR in June 1941, Polish citizens detained in the USSR were "amnestied," and a Polish army was established on the territory of the USSR. In 1942, about 120,000 people—soldiers of the newly created army and their families—were evacuated to Iran. These people were extensively interviewed about their experiences under the Soviet regime. The initiative to collect testimonial evidence came from the newly appointed Polish ambasaador to Moscow, Profesor Stanisław Kot, and was fully supported by the then commander of the Polish Army in the East, General Władysław Anders (the army is known colloquially as the "Anders Army"). Many questionnaires were distributed to the soldiers and their families. Surveys were conducted and the results later assembled by the Independent Historical Section of the Army, and then by the so-called Bureau of Documents. In April 1943 completed questionnaires were supposed to be transferred into the custody of civilian authorities in London, where the Polish government-in-exile resided. Some 12,000 protocols reached a Research Section established there under Professor Wiktor Sukiennicki.

For a fuller description and a study of Soviet occupation based on these materials, see my *Revolution from*

Abroad. Here I am referring to the county report for Łomża prepared by Professor Sukiennicki's staff, where references to Jedwabne can be found on pp. 14, 45, and 99. County reports and individual questionnaires can be found in the archives of the Hoover Institution in California, filed in two collections: the Polish Government Collection and the Anders Collection.

3. Janek Neumark, who was caught in 1939 in the area under the German occupation, returned to Jedwabne while it was still under the Soviet administration; he recalls his disappointment when he realized that the Soviets had confiscated a lot of property and arrested many Jews (*Yedwabne*, p. 112).

4. Majecki, typescript, p. 56. The author does not indicate his sources for this information. For an almost identical list of names—with the exception of Małyszew and the addition of a certain Afanasi Fedorovich Sobolev— see annex no. 3, "Wykaz obsady kadrowej radzieckich władz terenowych w regionie łomżyńskim w latach 1939–1941," in Michał Gniatowski, *W radzieckich okowach. Studium o agresji 17 września 1939r. i radzieckiej polityce w regionie łomżyńskim w latach 1939–1941* (Łomża: Łomżyńskie Towarzystwo Naukowe im. Wagów, 1997), p. 296.

5. For an analysis of this stereotype see my "A Tangled Web," in Deák, Gross, and Judt, *The Politics of Retribution in Europe*.

6. *Where Is My Older Brother Cain?*, pp. 158, 159.

7. Ibid., p. 491.

8. Krzysztof Jasiewicz, Tomasz Strzembosz, and Marek Wierzbicki eds., *Okupacja sowiecka (1939–1941) w świetle tajnych dokumentów* (Warsaw: ISP PAN, 1996), p. 212. Strzembosz has also written a long article entitled "Uroczysko Kobielno,"*Karta*, no. 5 (May–July 1991): 3– 27), in which he quotes excerpts from conversations, re-

corded in the 1980s, with participants in and proximate witnesses of these events. Gniatowski describes how this underground organization was destroyed by the NKVD (*W radzieckich okowach*, pp. 125–127).

9. I am grateful to Dr. Dariusz Stola for a very interesting suggestion as to how these two events might be linked: since the NKVD arrested a great number of people when they discovered the Kobielno underground organization, local elites could have been wiped out to the point that in July 1941 there remained no one with sufficient authority to stem the tide of anti-Jewish violence. There may be some truth in this hypothesis. However, Finkelsztajn's testimony from Radziłów, which I quote below, forces us to doubt whether local elites were willing to take a resolute stand opposing anti-Jewish violence in the area.

10. Borawski tells us that two of his brothers lived in Jedwabne. Since transliteration of some names from Wasersztajn's original testimony in Yiddish is imprecise, these might be the same as the Borowski or Borowiuk brothers mentioned by Wasersztajn.

11. Jan T. Gross and Irena G. Gross, eds., "*W czterdziestym nas matko na Sibir zesłali...*" (London: Aneks, 1983), pp. 330–332.

12. People interviewed by Strzembosz give some additional names of suspected informers and traitors, and none of them are Jewish (Strzembosz, "Uroczysko Kobielno," pp. 10, 11, 12, 15, 16, 19, 21). In his study of Polish-Jewish relations in western Belorussia Marek Wierzbicki writes that "in the years 1939–1941 the phenomenon of denunciation could also be found among the Polish population, especially in the ethnically Polish areas of the western part of the Białystok voivodeship" (Marek Wierzbicki, "Stosunki polsko-żydowskie na Zachodniej Białorusi (1939–1941). Rozważania wstępne" [manuscript, 1999–

2000], p. 15). Gniatowski cites numerical data from NKVD records indicating that there were no Jews in Polish underground organizations in this area (*W radzieckich okowach*, p. 120).

13. Jasiewicz, Strzembosz, and Wierzbicki, *Okupacja sowiecka (1939–1941)*, pp. 238–241. See also Gniatowski, *W radzieckich okowach*, p. 127.

THE OUTBREAK OF THE RUSSO-GERMAN WAR AND THE POGROM IN RADZIŁÓW

1. Conversation with Wiktor Niełacki, who as a sixteen-year-old fled to Jedwabne from Wizna, where scores of people had been murdered by the Germans immediately upon the occupying troops' arrival.

2. For a more extensive discussion of this subject see the chapter entitled "Collaboration" below.

3. Karol Bardoń's personality is more sharply delineated than that of any other accused in Ramotowski's trial. In part this is undoubtedly due to his writing ability: he could communicate much better than his codefendants, and he wrote more than others. But also, I think, he was a kinder man than the others; he expressed contrition for what he had done, and he seems to have had some sort of "bad luck" at various important junctures of his life. He drew the stiffest sentence of all the accused but was certainly not a key actor on the scene that day. I am even inclined to believe his claim that he barely appeared on the town square. He drew the death sentence because he was already in prison, sentenced to six years for serving as a uniformed German gendarme beginning in 1942.

His initial bad luck was to have been originally from Silesia and to have spoken fluent German since childhood. As a result he naturally became an intermediary between the Germans and the local population in Jedwabne and, in time, ended up in the German police force. His father was a socialist and worked as a clockmaker. Bardoń served in the Austro-Hungarian army in the First World War, then apprenticed as a mechanic in the clock factory, and was in and out of jobs until, in 1936, he settled in Jedwabne, where he maintained mechanical mills. From March 1939 Bardoń was unemployed again. At this time he had seven children to support (MC, SOŁ 123/496–499).

4. MC, SOŁ 123/499. Mieczysław Gerwad gives similar testimony: "When this area was taken over by germans, Czesław Kupiecki was beaten up by local people and delivered to the gendarmerie; they shot him together with a few other Jews. Who had beaten up and denounced Czesław Kupiecki to the gendarmerie I cannot tell, because I was not present there at the time, and these are the only details I later heard from people" (MC, SWB 145/34). And Julian Sokołowski, who was a little boy at the time, says, "I saw how citizen Kupiecki was standing near a wall with hands raised, and Germans beat him with rubber truncheons [gumą]. There were some Poles along with the Germans: citizen Kalinowski, presently dead after he was shot by the Security Office (UB) for being in a gang, also was beating Kupiecki" (MC, SWB 145/193). See also the decision in Ramotowski's appeal before the Supreme Court: MC, SOŁ 123/296.

5. Voivodeship Jewish Historical Commission in Białystok, 14.IV. 1946, testimony by Menachem Finkelsztajn, "Zagłada Żydów w powiecie grajewskim i łomżyńskim w lipcu 1941r," ŻIH. Finkelsztajn left several depositions concerning his experiences and what he knew about events of this period in Radziłów's vicinity. His second testimony, which I will quote at length, is entitled "Zburzenie gminy żydowskiej w Radziłowie."

6. ŽIH, 301/974. In his testimony published in Yiddish in the memorial book of Grajewo Jews, Finkelsztajn gives somewhat different details; he writes in the end that Radziłów Jews—after having been assembled in the square, where they had been beaten and many had been murdered—were brought to the outlying barn of a certain Mitkowski and burned there (*Grayeve yizker-bukh*, ed. G. Gorin, Hayman Blum, and Sol Fishbayn [New York: Aroysgegebn fun Fareyniktn Grayever hilfs-komitet, 1950], pp. 228–231). The script of the killing process provided by Finkelsztajn—initial murderous beatings of Jews assembled in the square followed by the herding of the entire community of some "sixty multigenerational families, including children, parents, and grandparents" into a barn where they were burned to death—is confirmed by an anonymous Pole interviewed by Andrzej Kaczyński for an article in *Rzeczpospolita*, July 10, 2000, "Nie zabijaj." I am grateful to attorney Jose Gutstein, a descendant of a Radziłów Jewish family, for making available to me an English translation of Finkelsztajn's Yiddish-language testimony.

7. *Rzeczpospolita*, July 10, 2000, "Nie zabijaj."

8. *Yedwabne*, p. 100. One of Niełáwicki's uncles went with the delegation to Łomża (conversation with Niełáwicki, February 2000). This episode is not without precedent. When murderous pogroms swept through the town of Lwów after the Germans arrived in the summer of 1941, the local rabbi visited the head of the Greek Catholic church there, Metropolite Andrzej Szeptycki, to plead for an end to the pogroms.

PREPARATIONS

1. During his trial Sobuta maintained that he had no official function in the town hall and went there only occasionally to do repair work. But several witnesses de-

scribe him as Karolak's "deputy," or as a "secretary" of the town council (see, for instance, depositions of Ramotowski and Gerwad in MC, SWB 145/217, 226). Sobuta was pronounced not guilty in his trial because, as explained earlier, he could not be associated with the death of Kupiecki. But there was abundant evidence of his leading role in the murder of Jedwabne Jews. In the testimonies of witnesses and accused in Ramotowski's trial his name appears in depositions, among others, by Ramotowski, Górski, Niebrzydowski, Laudański, Miciura, Chrzanowski, and Dąbrowski (MC, SOŁ 123/610, 611, 615, 618, 653, 655).

2. Both the Pecynowicz brothers and Olszewicz's parents ignored warnings from their children and nephews. The older generation somehow could not accept that the end of the world could come at any moment. Young people spent this night in the fields, and by early dawn they saw peasants coming into town on foot and in carts, an occurrence ordinarily limited to market days. A while later the pogrom began (*Yedwabne*, p. 100; conversation with M. Olszewicz, October 1999).

3. MC, SWB 145/218.

4. MC, SOŁ 123/665.

5. MC, SWB 145/506.

6. "Eugeniusz Śliwecki was then deputy mayor, and together with the mayor signed an agreement with the gestapo to burn the jews. . . . That such an agreement was signed by the mayor and the deputy mayor I only heard from people" (MC, SWB 145/213). I would like to point out that the circumstances of the July 10, 1941, mass murder of the Jews were a frequent topic of conversation in town. As a result people are knowledgeable about details that they did not necessarily witness in person. "The local population spoke very often about the murder of jews in Śleszyński's barn, and they told each other who was most

prominent in this murder," writes, for example, Henryk Krystowczyk (MC, SWB 145/235). Even today one can easily get people (who for the most part were born well after the war) talking about these events in a Jedwabne bar (see also Andrzej Kaczyński's article "Całopalenie" in *Rzeczpospolita*, May 5, 2000). It seems to me that in a village where people keep telling each other who murdered how many Jews, and in what manner, hardly any room is left for conversation on any other subject. Citizens of Jedwabne would thus have been cursed with a "Midas touch" condemning them to a perpetual preoccupation with Jews (whom they had wanted to get rid of once and for all), and with murder. Antosia Wyrzykowska says that when she visited the town, many years after the war, she was still scared.

7. We can only speculate about a certain aspect of these conversations reported in testimonies by Wasersztajn and Grądowski (who merely repeat what they overheard, as they did not participate in these conversations)—namely, whether, indeed, the Germans suggested that some Jewish craftsmen be kept alive, and were dissuaded by Bronisław Śleszyński's argument that there were enough skilled craftsmen among the Poles. Nielawicki, who escaped from the Jewish crowd on the way to the barn, mentions another variation of this story, according to which the Germans are said to have made their point near the barn. It was there, allegedly, that one of the Polish organizers promised to deliver all the labor force that might be needed in the future, made up exclusively of Poles (conversation with Nielawicki, February 2000). The story is also confirmed—also as hearsay, however—by an elderly Polish peasant, Leon Dziedzic, in an interview with Adam Wilma printed in *Gazeta Pomorska* on August 4, 2000.

8. The number is given by Bardoń, who worked at the gendarmerie outpost and later became a gendarme

(*Schutzmann*) himself. Nieławicki estimated the size of the police force in town to be about ten (MC, SOŁ123/505; conversation with Nieławicki, February 2000).

9. MC, SOŁ 123/621.

10. MC, SOŁ 123/607.

11. MC, SOŁ 123/612.

12. MC, SOŁ 123/619.

13. As Józef Danowski put it during a confrontation staged by the Security Office between him and Sobuta in 1953, "Germans also took part in this action, but only by issuing [orders], or rather expressing consent for various decisions during this action" (MC, SWB 145/265).

WHO MURDERED THE JEWS OF JEDWABNE?

1. MC, SOŁ 123/685.

2. MC, SOŁ 123/727.

3. MC, SWB 145/218.

4. MC, SOŁ 123/630.

5. MC, SOŁ 123/631. Bardoń (see below), Nieławicki, and Kubran confirm that Jews were saved at the gendarmerie outpost (*Yedwabne*, p. 107; conversation with Nieławicki, February 2000). Nieławicki also confirms that firearms were not used during the pogrom, and that people in uniform were not seen among the murderers.

6. MC, SOŁ 123/210.

7. Wiarus's outfit "entered the town of Jedwabne. The local militia outpost was forced to defend itself. During this time Wiarus's people robbed the local cooperative, the town council, and the post office. During this action one of the members of the group made a short speech to the people of Jedwabne calling on them to fight against the government" (Henryk Majecki, *Białostocczyzna w pier-*

wszych latach władzy ludowej 1944–1948 [Warsaw: PWN, 1977], p. 181).

8. After the war various anti-German guerrilla detachments continued their activities, directed now against the Communist Party–sponsored state authorities. Detachments of NSZ (National Armed Forces), NOW (National Military Organization), and NZW (National Military Association) that were active in this region killed numerous Jews, communists, and other people whom they considered undesirable. In Frączek's doctoral dissertation ("Formacje zbrojne obozu narodowego na Białostocczyźnie w latach 1939–1956"), quoted earlier, we find ample information on this aspect of their postwar activities (see pp. 150–151, 187, 194, 254, 297). Among other executions we know that in Jedwabne an outfit commanded by "Sęp" killed Julia Karolak, who owned a store in town, and her daughter on September 24, 1945 (p. 385). Whether this was a botched robbery or some settling of scores we cannot now determine, but any inhabitant of this town must have been aware long after the war of the anticommunist underground's propensity for carrying out "punishment," including executions. As Tomasz Strzembosz puts it, "In this territory . . . war did not last five or six years (1939–1944, 1939–1945) but rather ten years or even thirteen (1939–1949, 1939–1952), and in certain places even longer. . . . Not far from Biebrza's riverbank and the village of Jedwabne there is a small hamlet, Jeziorko; it was there that an epigon, with the pseudonym 'Ryba,' of the Białystok-region guerrillas was killed in 1957" (Strzembosz, "Uroczysko Kobielno," p. 5).

9. MC, SOŁ 123/309. Bardoń describes this episode in more detail in his autobiography, written in 1952. He states that this took place in the evening when the barn was already on fire. Suddenly in the courtyard of the gendar-

merie "there showed up three civilians, unknown to me, young men twenty-two years old—one grabbed a woodchopper and took him by force to the square; two other murderers were trying to take two other woodchoppers. Hearing screams in the courtyard, the commander of the post, *Hauptwachmeister* Adamy, ran out and said those words to these hoodlums: 'So—eight hours was not enough to do away with the Jews, and you also had to come here. Get out of here!' He chased away these criminals; the two choppers remained; the third one was already taken" (MC, SOŁ 123/504, 505).

10. Preceding this passage Bardoń writes the following: "I was working with Dombrowski the entire day in the courtyard, and I did not see even one unfamiliar gendarme or Gestapo man" (MC, SOŁ 123/506).

11. Józef Sobuta and eight of the accused in the Ramotowski trial.

12. One Czesław Lipiński, for example, tells us, "I sat with this cane [on the square] for about fifteen minutes, but I couldn't watch how they were murdering them, and I went home." But he must have stopped somewhere along the way to participate in the day's atrocities, for it is unlikely that in this trial one could be sentenced to ten years in prison for spending fifteen minutes sitting with "a cane" in the square (MC, SOŁ 123/607).

13. MC, SOŁ 123/655.

14. MC, SOŁ 123/668.

15. MC, SOŁ 123/726.

16. MC, SOŁ 123/620.

17. *Where Is My Older Brother Cain?*, p. 490. An elderly woman, Bronisława Kalinowska, stated on the witness stand in Ramotowski's trial, "In 1941, when the German occupiers' army entered the territory of the town of Jedwabne, the local population began to murder the Jews, and

one couldn't really watch how they tortured the Jews" (MC, SOŁ 123/686). When I spoke with Mrs. Adamczyk in Jedwabne (October 1999), who as a little girl was not let out of the house on that day, she grabbed her head in a dramatic gesture at the recollection of the frightening sounds of screaming people and a horrible stench of burning bodies (see also the previously mentioned article "Całopalenie," in the May 5, 2000, issue of *Rzeczpospolita*).

18. Adam Wilma, "Broda mojego syna," *Gazeta Pomorska*, August 4, 2000.

THE MURDER

1. An illustration of how a small-town population behaved under such circumstances is the April 13, 1942, entry from the *Dziennik lat okupacji zamojszczyzny* (Lublin: Ludowa Spółdzielnia Wydawnicza, 1958) by Zygmunt Klukowski: "There is even more panic among the Jews. From the morning on they were expecting the gendarmes and the Gestapo. . . . All kinds of lowlifes crawled out about the town; many horse carts came from the countryside, and all of them were waiting the whole day in anticipation, awaiting the moment they could start the plundering. From various directions we get news about scandalous behavior of the Polish population, about plundering of abandoned Jewish dwellings. In this respect our village certainly will not lag behind" (p. 255). On the phenomenon of a "pogrom wave," see n. 1 on pp. 235–236, describing a wave of pogroms that in 1919 swept the vicinity of Kolbuszowa. Concerning the participation of the same people in subsequent pogroms, see also Finklesztajn's testimony about the events in Radziłów.

2. I am quoting from Danowski's testimony in August 1953 (MC, SWB, 145/238). In his testimony of December 31, 1952, he mentions the distribution of vodka in

front of the town hall. We know from trial documents that Danowski was an alcoholic. Quite possibly, then, the free vodka was a detail that was sharply carved in his memory (MC, SWB 145/185, 186, 279).

3. *Yedwabne*, p. 102. People knew from past experience that their houses, when left unattended, might be broken into. Nieławicki, for example, running into the fields on this day, put on two good pairs of trousers and two shirts, expecting to find the house plundered upon his return. We know also from Laudański that Jews were assembled on the square under the pretext of a cleaning job.

4. Ibid., p. 103.

5. MC, SOŁ 123/503.

6. MC, SOŁ 123/734.

7. MC, SOŁ 123/503.

8. MC, SOŁ 123/503, 504.

9. MC SOŁ 123/683.

10. MC, SOŁ 123/675.

11. *Yedwabne*, p. 103.

12. ŻIH, 301/613.

13. MC, SOŁ 123/675; ŻIH, 301/613 (this is the second deposition by Wasersztajn). When I asked Nieławicki what he observed when he was brought to the square, he told me that he did not look around much but rather tried to move into the center of the crowd because it was encircled by a tight ring of people wielding clubs and other blunt instruments, beating anyone within reach (conversation with Nieławicki, February 2000). Several witnesses already quoted have this merciless beating of Jews in the square in mind when they say that this was a spectacle "one could not look at."

14. MC, SOŁ 123/681.

15. ŻIH, 301/613.

16. MC, SOŁ 123/686.

17. MC, SOŁ 123/614.

18. MC, SOŁ 123/653.

19. MC, SWB 145/255. In addition to Adam Grabowski other witnesses, as well as perpetrators, offer the same description of this episode. Thus Julian Sokołowski states: "I remember that when jews were chased [toward the barn], citizen Sobuta gave his stick to the rabbi and ordered him to put his hat on it and scream, 'War is because of us, war is for us.' All this crowd of jews on the way toward the barn outside town was screaming, 'War is because of us, war is for us' " (MC, SWB 145/192); see also testimonies by Jerzy Laudański (MC, SOŁ 123/665); Stanisław Danowski (MC, SWB 145/186); and Zygmunt Laudański (MC, SOŁ 123/667).

20. MC, SOŁ 123/666.

21. *Yedwabne*, p. 103.

22. MC, SOŁ 123/618. Bardoń also played some part in this transaction of "releasing" kerosene from the warehouse—of which he may have been in charge as a mechanic. But he states in his testimony that he ordered Niebrzydowski to issue kerosene "for technical purposes and not to burn a barn full of people" (MC, SOŁ 123/505).

23. *Yedwabne*, p. 113.

24. *Rzeczpospolita*, July 10, 2000, "Nie zabijaj."

25. MC, SOŁ 123/685. See also the testimony of Władysław Miciura, who says, "From further away I saw only Józef Kobrzeniecki, who was setting the barn on fire" (MC, SOŁ 123/655).

26. MC, SOŁ 123/684.

27. MC, SOŁ 123/734.

28. MC, SOŁ 123/506.

29. *Rzeczpospolita*, July 10, 2000, "Nie zabijaj."

30. Adam Wilma, "Broda mojego syna," *Gazeta Pomorska*, August 4, 2000.

PLUNDER
   1. MC, SOŁ 123/631, 632, 675, 676, 677, 682, 683.
   2. MC, SWB 145/168.
   3. MC, SWB 145/164, 165.
   4. MC, SWB 145/253. Sobuta, of course, denied that he had taken any Jewish property. "After the murder of the Jewish population I began to occupy a leftover Jewish apartment because I did not have my own. When I entered the leftover Jewish apartment, there weren't any furnishings or any other things there, and so I do not have anything of the sort. All leftover Jewish things were brought to the town hall, and I don't know what happened with them later" (MC, SWB 145/267).

It is worth noting that the phenomenon of appropriating other people's belongings is coded into language. The words *pożydowski* and *poniemiecki* are immediately understandable to a native speaker of Polish as "leftover Jewish," or "leftover German," property. If, on the other hand, by analogy an expression *poangielski* or *pofrancuski* was used, a native speaker would assume that whoever uttered those words had made a mistake—a Russianism, to be exact—and should have used *po angielsku* or *po francusku* instead. Those expressions mean "in the English (or in the French) language," and one could not use them to designate leftover French or English property. Simply put, owing to accidents of history, the Jews and the Germans were the only peoples whose belongings the Poles have ever appropriated.

   5. MC, SWB 145/165.
   6. MC, SOŁ 123/728.
   7. For reference to Karolak, see n. 5 on pp. 209–210. The Laudańskis are mentioned in the document entitled "Do Komitetu Centralnego P.P.R. w Warszawie." It was received in the Central Control Commission of the Central Committee of the Communist Party on October 2, 1948,

and then undoubtedly passed on to the security service—it is currently in the control-investigative files of the Łomża Security Office (UOP).

8. In the May 19, 2000, issue of *Rzeczpospolita*, the second most important daily in Poland after *Gazeta Wyborcza*, Andrzej Kaczyński thus concludes his excellent second piece of investigative reporting, "Oczyszczanie pamięci," on the massacre of Jews in Jedwabne.

INTIMATE BIOGRAPHIES

1. MC, SOŁ 123/718.
2. MC, SOŁ 123/712.
3. MC, SOŁ 123/498.
4. MC, SOŁ 123/273–274.
5. This lengthy characterization of Jerzy Laudański can be found in a document entitled "Arkusz informacyjny 'dossier' na podejrzanych o przestępstwa przeciwko Państwu," held with other control-investigative materials of the Łomża Public Security Office in the Białystok archives of the UOP.
6. MC, SOŁ 123/809.
7. MC, SOŁ 123/702.

ANACHRONISM

1. Here, for example, is a description of events that "broke out in the spring of 1919 in the eastern part of former Western Galicia. Enormous and bestially brutal [*potężne i bestialskie*] anti-Jewish peasant movements took place there, reminiscent of the 'slaughter and plunder' that overwhelmed the same territory under a movement led by Jakub Szela in the spring of 1846." I am quoting here from an article by a history teacher and local patriot from the town of Kolbuszowa, who was not especially sympathetic to the Jews. "Huge crowds of peasants gathered at the time,

men, women, and young people; they rode on carts from town to town armed with truncheons, and beat up and plundered the Jews, robbing their businesses and homes. . . . . In those days Polish Catholics believed," the author continues, "that Jews who hated Catholics and called them 'goyim' added a little blood of Catholic children to their matzoh. . . . It is not known how this belief originated, but it was there, and Catholic mothers used to discipline their unruly children by invoking it, telling their children, in other words, that Jews would kill them if they misbehaved. [I remember being disciplined by my nanny, who used to say that Gypsies would kidnap me if I did not mend my ways]. In Glinik a girl disappeared, and a peasant crowd assaulted Jewish homes, beating and even killing the Jews and plundering their businesses and their houses. Such shocking news [i.e., that a girl had been killed by the Jews for matzoh] quickly spread among inhabitants in the countryside over vast territories and resulted in enormous, aggressive, and very cruel actions by peasants [*olbrzymie i agresywne, niezmiernie okrutne, akcje chłopskie*]. Beginning on May 1, [1919], big groups armed with truncheons, axes, pitchforks, and other similar instruments assaulted Jewish homes . . . resulting in pogroms and huge plunder" (Halina Dudzińska, "Kolbuszowa i kolbuszowianie w okresie narodzin II Rzeczypospolitej Polskiej i walki o ustalenie jej granic," *Rocznik Kolbuszowski*, no. 3 [Kolbuszowa, 1994]: 129).

2. The pogrom, which lasted for almost an entire day (July 4, 1946), involved the participation of hundreds of Kielce inhabitants and resulted in the murder of forty-two Jews. It began with a made-up accusation by a young boy who, at the instigation of his father, declared that he had been held captive for a few days in the basement of a building where Jewish survivors and returnees lived in

Kielce (presumably in order to have his blood harvested in a ritual murder)—incidentally, there was no basement in this building. A squad of Citizens' Militia (MO) was then dispatched to search the house and investigate the matter, and the pogrom started. Both militiamen and uniformed soldiers were involved in the killings. There was certainly massive incompetence on the part of security forces in the way they responded to unfolding events—maybe even foul play. The main point debated by Polish historians and journalists addressing the subject (to the extent that they did so at all, for the matter was considered taboo during the communist rule) was whether this had been deliberately provoked by the security police. The best study of the Kielce pogrom can be found in Bożena Szaynok's *Pogrom Żydów w Kielcach 4 VII 1946 r.* (Warsaw: Wydawnictwo Bellona, 1991). For a well-documented study of the pogrom in Cracow, see a Jagiellonian University unpublished M.A. thesis by Anna Cichopek, "Z dziejów powojennego antysemityzmu—pogrom w Krakowie 11 sierpnia 1945r." (Cracow, 1998).

3. "Lately," wrote the chairman of the Jewish Committee in Częstochowa, Brener, in August 1946, "an eleven-year-old Christian child walked with his mother down Garibaldi Street, where many Jews are living, and pointed to a house where Jews had allegedly held him for two days. This time Christian neighbors ridiculed the boy and chased him away. . . . Even though the danger is almost gone, and people's minds are beginning to settle down, this episode made a terrible impression on our neighborhood. People started to close down their businesses and lock up their apartments, and prepared to flee. Where to? Nobody knows and nobody can tell" (*Głos Bundu*, no. 1 [Warsaw, August 1946]). See also *Upiorna dekada*, pp. 104, 105.

WHAT DO PEOPLE REMEMBER?

1. Aharon Appelfeld, "Buried Homeland," *New Yorker*, November 23, 1998, pp. 48, 51, 52.

2. Ibid., p. 54.

3. In Hochberg-Mariańska's introduction to a 1947 book of personal testimonies by Jewish children who survived the war, we read that several Poles who had helped Jews during the war requested anonymity for fear of hostile reactions in their own communities if their wartime deeds became known (Maria Hochberg-Mariańska's introduction to *Dzieci oskarżają* (Cracow: Centralna Żydowska Komisja Historyczna w Polsce, 1947). This was a general phenomenon. See also, for example, Nechama Tec's memoir *Dry Tears: The Story of a Lost Childhood* (New York: Oxford University Press, 1984). It is a fascinating subject—why were those who would come to be honored as Righteous Amongst Nations afraid of their own neighbors, should those neighbors find out that they had helped Jews during the war? There were two reasons, I believe. In the first place they feared becoming robbery victims. In popular imagination Jews were associated with money, and people were persuaded that all those who sheltered Jews during the war must thereby have enriched themselves. But there was another reason as well. The future Righteous's wartime behavior broke the socially approved norm, demonstrating that they were different from everybody else and, therefore, a danger to the community. They were a threat to others because, potentially, they could bear witness. They could tell what had happened to local Jews because they were not—whether by their deeds or by their reluctance to act— bonded into a community of silence over this matter.

4. The underground, as explained in n. 8 on p. 229, continued its existence well past the end of the hostilities against the Germans.

5. The Wyrzykowskis' nephew, Jarosław Karwowski, wrote down this deposition in Milanówek on May 2, 1962 (ŻIH, 301/5825, conversation with Wyrzykowska, October 1999).

COLLECTIVE RESPONSIBILITY

1. Richard Breitman, *The Architect of Genocide: Himmler and the Final Solution* (New York: Alfred Knopf, 1991), pp. 171–173.

2. "Maria had to make a phone call. We entered a small pastry shop as she thought there was a telephone there. It turned out otherwise however; there was no telephone. Faced with this situation Maria decided to leave me there alone for a few minutes, she bought me a pastry, chose the least visible table in a fairly dark corner, and told me she would return right away, as soon as she took care of the phone call. She told the same thing to the woman who'd serve us, undoubtedly the shopowner. . . . I ate my pastry and what the women (there were no men) were chatting about amongst themselves didn't concern me. Yet after a while I couldn't not realize that things were playing out otherwise. It was difficult to harbor any doubts that I'd found myself in the center of attention. The women—perhaps shop assistants, perhaps clients—had gathered around the shopowner, whispering and at the same time observing me intently. I was already sufficiently experienced as a Jewish child in hiding so as to understand at once what this meant and what this could foreshadow. . . .

"I felt their observation of me palpably. . . . The women stared at me as if I were an extraordinary monster, whose very existence called into question the laws of nature. And as if in a moment they would have to decide what to do with me, for things couldn't stay as they were . . . , I heard: 'A Jew, there's no question, a Jew' . . . 'She certainly isn't, but he—a Jew' . . . 'She's foisted him off onto us.' . . . The women deliberated what to do with me. The shopowner opened the doors leading to the back room, where the kitchen must have been, and called out: 'Hela, Hela, come and look.' And after a while this Hela appeared, in an apron covered with flour, obviously interrupted from her work. They waited for her judgment, clearly they counted on her opinion. Perhaps she was an authority in various matters, or even an expert in racial questions—within the context of the pastry shop, which for me had ceased to be a calm and quiet place. In any case one more pair of piercing eyes arrived to examine me. . . .

"There was no escape from the understanding that my situation was growing worse from moment to moment. The women were no longer satisfied with observing me from afar. . . . Perhaps they wanted confirmation, some final justification for the decision they would reach (and quite possibly already had reached). For I heard one of them say: 'We have to call the police.'

"The women having discussed the matter and their curiosity now aroused, came nearer, they approached the table where I was sitting. And so began the interrogation. First one of them asked my name. I had false papers, I'd learned my identity—and I answered politely. Another was curious about my relationship to the woman who'd brought me here—I answered again, this time truthfully. . . . They continued to shower me with questions: what my parents were doing, where was I from, where I had been recently, where I was going . . . and so forth. They tried to pose their questions gently, sometimes even sweetly. I wasn't deceived by their tone, however, for after all it required no great perspicacity to sense that behind that tone lurked fury and aggression. They spoke to me as to a child—and yet at once as to a defendant or even an outright criminal. Now that years have passed, I don't believe that they were driven by pure resentment or hatred. Rather they dreaded the problem which had suddenly fallen into their laps and were prepared to do anything—by all possible means and at whatever price—in order to rid themselves of it as quickly as possible. . . .

"The women asked me various questions, to which by then I'd ceased to respond, rather muttering sometimes only 'yes' or 'no.' . . . Yet I heard not only the questions directed at me but also the comments the women expressed more quietly, to the side, as if only to themselves, but in such a way that I couldn't fail to hear. Most often they spit out the threatening word 'Jew,' but also, most terrifying, they repeated: 'we have to call the police.' I was aware that this was equivalent to a death sentence. . . . Those women were not possessed by an uncontrollable hatred. . . . These were normal, ordinary, in their own way resourceful and decent women, hard-working, undoubtedly scrambling to take care of their families in the difficult conditions under the occupation. Neither would I exclude the possibility that they were exemplary mothers and wives, perhaps religious, possessing a whole array of virtues. They had found themselves in a situation that to them felt troublesome and threatening, and so they wanted to face it directly. They did not think, though, at what price. Perhaps that transcended their imaginations—although they must have known how it would end if they were to 'call them'—or perhaps it was simply not within the boundaries of the moral reflection accessible to them" (Michał Głowiński, "Kwardans spędzony w cukierni," in *Czarne Sezony* [Warsaw: Open, 1998], pp. 93–95; translated by Marci Shore).

3. Michał Cichy, "Polacy-Żydzi: czarne karty Powstania Warszawskiego," *Gazeta Wyborcza*, January 29–30, 1994.

NEW APPROACH TO SOURCES

1. In 1987 an eminent literary scholar, Jan Błoński, published a thoughtful essay entitled "The Poor Poles Look at the Ghetto" (the title alludes to Czesław Miłosz's poem "The Poor Christians Look at the Ghetto"), where he suggested that Poles shared *responsibility* for the genocide of Jews. He introduced an important distinction by specifically disclaiming Polish *participation* in the attrocities. As he put it: "One can share the responsibility for the crime without taking part in it. Our responsibility is for holding back, for insufficient effort to resist." The venerable Catholic weekly *Tygodnik Powszechny* in which the essay appeared was overwhelmed with letters of protest from its readers and was compelled to publish "A Reply to Jan Błoński" authored by a distinguished attorney, who had in the past defended several oppositionists in political trials and had himself been sentenced to death by a Stalinist court in the 1950s. On this occasion he felt compelled to defend "the good name" of his compatriots, who were collectively libeled, he believed, by Błoński's argument. The essays by Jan Błoński and Władysław Siła-Nowicki, together with several other articles published as a follow-up to Błoński's essay and a discussion on these matters held at a conference in Jerusalem one year later are collected in an English-language volume, *"My Brother's Keeper?" Recent Polish Debates on the Holocaust*, ed. Antony Polonsky (London: Routledge, 1990).

IS IT POSSIBLE TO BE SIMULTANEOUSLY
A VICTIM AND A VICTIMIZER?

1. See my article "A Tangled Web," in Deák, Gross, and Judt, *The Politics of Retribution in Europe*.

2. Atina Grossman, "Trauma, Memory, and Motherhood: Germans and Jewish Displaced Persons in Post-

Nazi Germany, 1945–1949," *Archiv für Sozialgeschichte* 38 (1998): 215–239, especially its opening section, "Introduction: Different Voices on 'Armes Deutschland,' " pp. 215–217. See also an early Hannah Arendt article, "The Aftermath of Nazi Rule," *Commentary*, October 1950, pp. 342–353.

There were also other grounds that could serve to instill a sense of victimization among the Germans, in particular the widespread and recurrent rape of German women by the soldiers of the Red Army, and the fate of refugees and expellees from East Prussia, Silesia, and the Sudetenland. See Norman Naimark, *The Russians in Germany: A History of the Soviet Zone of Occupation, 1945–1949* (Cambridge: Harvard University Press, Belknap Press, 1995).

3. For a good aperçu concerning the personalities of "old Communists," and Jakub Berman (1901–1984) and Hilary Minc (1905–1974) in particular, see the volume of interviews published by Teresa Torańska, *Oni: Stalin's Polish Puppets* (London: Collins Harvill, 1987). Both of these men came from Jewish families and rose to prominence in the Communist Party apparatus during the war, which they spent in the Soviet Union. In late forties and early fifties they were in the politburo of the Polish Communist Party, where Berman was responsible for the security apparatus and Minc for control over the economy.

4. Łukasz Kamiński, *Strajki robotnicze w Polsce w latach 1945–1948* (Wrocław: GAIT Wydawnictwo s.c., 1999).

5. See n. 2 on pp. 236–237 for a brief note about circumstances surrounding the Kielce pogrom.

6. Kamiński, *Strajki robotnicze w Polsce w latach 1945–1948*, p. 46.

7. Quoted in Gross, "A Tangled Web," in Deák, Gross, and Judt, *The Politics of Retribution in Europe* p. 111.

8. *Yedwabne*, p. 98.

COLLABORATION

1. For a brief, contextualized history of the application of this concept, see my "Social History of War and Occupation in Europe," in Deák, Gross, and Judt, *The Politics of Retribution in Europe*, pp. 23–32.

2. Krystyna Kersten, *Narodziny systemu władzy. Polska 1943–1948* (Paryż: Libella, 1986), p. 172.

3. Both quotations are from manuscripts submitted in 1948 to a competition inviting memoirs and recollections concerning what happened during the decade of war in one's village. It was organized by the publishing house Czytelnik. All the submissions were published a quarter century later in four volumes entitled *Wieś polska 1939–1948, materiały konkursowe*, ed. Krystyna Kersten and Tomasz Szarota (Warsaw: PWN, 1971). The two excerpts I quote were deleted by the state's Censors' Office and did not appear in print. I have been provided access to the original submissions by Professor Tomasz Szarota, who directs the Laboratory of Polish History after 1945 at the Polish Academy of Sciences, where these materials are deposited. I am very grateful for his assistance.

Incidentally, one wonders at the complete openness of simple people who in 1948 sent to an official institution their recollections, which were so out of synch with the officially approved version of current events. The quotations above can be found in manuscripts no. 20 (931), p. 4, and 72 (1584), p. 5.

In another source—the catalog of the well-known photographic exhibit about the Wehrmacht's participation in the killings of Jews on the Eastern Front (*The German*

Army and the Genocide, ed. Hamburg Institute for Social Research [New York: The New Press, 1999], p. 81)—we find a beautiful photograph of a German soldier on a motorcycle surrounded by a group of smiling young women who offer him food and drink. The caption reads, "Ukrainian women offer refreshments." This perfectly matches the official Soviet iconography of the reception the Red Army received when it was "liberating" these territories in September 1939.

Another interesting documentation of the friendly reception the Wehrmacht received in the summer of 1941 as it advanced across these territories can be found in the documentary film by Ruth Beckermann entitled *East of War*. She visited the above-mentioned exhibit when it opened in Vienna and interviewed on camera older men who happened to be at the show. These were for the most part Wehrmacht veterans, who told her fascinating stories.

4. Here is an excerpt, for example, from the *Ereignismeldung UdSSR* no. 21, dated July 13, 1941, referring specifically to the situation in Białystok: "The executions continue all the time at the same rate. The Polish section of the population has shown that it supports the executions by the Security Police by informing on Jewish, Russian, and also Polish Bolsheviks" (*Einsatzgruppen Reports*, p. 23).

5. I have covered this subject extensively in "A Tangled Web," in Deák, Gross, and Judt, *The Politics of Retribution in Europe*.

6. Eric Voegelin, *Hitler and the Germans* (Columbia: University of Missouri Press, 1999), p. 105.

7. Kazimierz Wyka, *Życie na niby. Pamiętnik po klęsce* (Cracow: Wydawnictwo Literackie, 1984).

8. Both quotations are from Białystok voivodeship: "The population of my hamlet and its vicinity got completely demoralized during nine years of war. People

stopped working. A new saying came into usage: Let the stupid one work; I will manage by hook or by crook [*ja będę kombinował*]. And they managed by brewing thousands of liters of hooch." Another peasant, recalling the period of Soviet occupation in the village of Kroszówka in Grajewo County, adjacent to Jedwabne, gave the following sketch of neighborly relations: "Drinking on a grand scale began in the village, drinking bouts, fights, robberies. Everybody who quarreled or had some old scores to settle went to the office and said that this one and that one was 'political' before the war. Arrests began, and people got fearful, not knowing what they might be arrested for" (Kersten and Szarota, *Wieś polska 1939–1948, materiały konkursowe*, pp. 125, 66).

     9. ŻIH, 301/579.

     10. Klukowski, *Dziennik z lat okupacji zamojszczyzny*, p. 299.

     11. In a report sent to London on December 8, 1939, from the territories occupied by the Soviets we read, "Jews are so horribly persecuting the Poles and everything that is connected to Poland under the Soviet occupation . . . that at the first opportunity all the Poles, from old men to women and children, will take such a horrible revenge on them as no antisemite has ever imagined possible" (Gross, *Upiorna dekada*, p. 92). As a description of reality this text was wrong, but as a forecast of things to come it was prescient.

SOCIAL SUPPORT FOR STALINISM

     1. Let me quote Voegelin again on this point: "[O]ur problem is that a useless man exists at all levels of society up to its highest ranks . . . so I would suggest the neutral expression 'rabble' for this. There are men who are rabble in the sense that they neither have the authority of

spirit or of reason, nor are they able to respond to reason or spirit, if it emerges advising or reminding them. . . . it is extremely difficult to understand that the elite of a society can consist of rabble. But it really does consist of rabble" (*Hitler and the Germans*, p. 89).

2. On the flight of Jewish survivors after the war from small towns or rural areas toward large urban centers, see, for example, Gross, *Upiorna dekada*, pp. 102, 103.

3. A devastating, contemporaneous record of undisguised antisemitism practiced by Communist Party activists in Poland preceding and during the so-called March events in 1968 has been provided by Mieczysław Rakowski in his *Political Journals* (*Dzienniki polityczne, 1967–1968* (Warsaw: Iskry, 1999). Rakowski was a member of the Central Committee of the Polish United Workers' Party at the time, and editor in chief of the best opinion weekly in the Soviet bloc, *Polityka*. Thus he really had a front-row seat from which to document the mechanisms of the "anti-Zionist campaign" of 1967–1968, as it was called in the official media.

INDEX

Adamy, 102–103

Anders Army questionnaires, 43

antisemitism: assigning responsibility for, 133–135; collective memory on events of, 122–123, 235n.1; "leftover" Jewish property motive for, 105–107, 110, 234n.4; link between sovietization and, 164–167; Polish moral disintegration and, 157–163; post–World War II Polish, 150–151, 247n.3; ritual murder belief and, 123–124, 150, 236n.1; sources of violent, 123–125; vulnerable to outbursts of, 38–39. *See also* Jewish pogroms

anti-Soviet underground (Jedwabne), 47–53

Appelfeld, Aharon, 126–128

Arendt, Hannah, 4

Armes Deutschland ("Poor Germany") response, 144–145

Arnold, Agnieszka, 22, 24, 37, 46, 88, 171, 211n.7

Baker, Rabbi Jacob, 37

Bardoń, Karol: clemency petition filed by, 83–85, 111; confessional text by, 113–114; German collaboration by, 117; Jedwabne massacre described by, 56, 92–93, 95; Jedwabne massacre role by, 94, 102; Jewish property taken by, 106; massacre role by, 233n.22; personality and

Bardoń, Karol *(cont.)*
  background of, 223n.3;
  on visit of Gestapo to
  Jedwabne, 75
Białystok District Committee
  of the CP(b)B, 52
Białostocki, Rabbi Avigdor,
  39, 40
Binsztajn, Baśia, 17
Borawski, Antoni, 48–52
Borowiuk (Borowski?), Mie-
  tek, 18
Borowiuk (Borowski?),
  Waclaw, 18
Borowski (Borwiuk?), Wacek,
  16
Browning, Christopher, 120
Brzozowska, Betka, 96
BSSR (Belorussian Soviet So-
  cialist Republic), 115. *See
  also* Soviet occupation
  (1939–1941)
Bystrov, Piotr Ivanovich, 44

"Całopalenie" (Kaczyński),
  171
Catholic clergy, 219n.9
Chrzanowski, Józef, 98, 106
Cichy, Michał, 137
collaboration: alleged Jewish-
  Soviet, 10–11, 46–47, 155,
  246n.11; Borawski testimony on Soviet, 49–51; conventional wisdom on *szmalcownicy*, 8; defining, 205n.3;
  denunciation phenomenon
  and, 222n.12; *fuite en avant*

and, 117; historiography regarding *szmalcownicy*, 8, 139,
  207n.10; by Jedwabne massacre participants, 16–20,
  115–118, 163; Laudański's
  (Zygmunt) petition describing, 114–117; totalitarian
  logic of incentives for, 117–
  118; World War II context
  of, 5
Communist Party of Western
  Belorussia, 44
Cooperative of Peasant Self-
  Help, 116
Cracow pogrom (1945), 149–
  150
Czytelnik memoir contest
  (1948), 157–158, 244n.3

Dąbrowski, 49–50
Danowski testimony, 91,
  231n.2
Deák, Istvan, 6
denunciation phenomenon,
  222n.12
Dobrzańska, 96
documentation: by Aleksander
  Wyrzykowski, 130–131; Anders Army questionnaires,
  43; Borawski's testimony,
  49–51; used to challenge
  Jedwabne massacre historiography, 138–142; critical
  appraisal of, 27–28; *Ereignismeldung UdSSR* reports,
  211n.1; on prewar Jed-
  wabne, 218n.2; Ringelblum

Archive, 213n.4; Wasersztajn deposition, 15–22, 24, 97, 101, 140. *See also* Jedwabne massacre documentation; Jedwabne massacre trial; Jewish testimonies

Dolegowski, Father Aleksander, 62–63

Dubnow, Simon, 25

Dziedzic, Leon, 103

Dziekoński, Henryk, 61

Dziennik z lat okupacji zamojszczyzny (Klukowski), 161–162

Einsatzgruppen (German police detachments), 23–24, 132

Ereignismeldung UdSSR reports, 211n.1, 245n.4

"final solution." *See* Holocaust

Finkelsztajn, Menachem, 57–69, 141, 155, 224n.5, 225n.6

Fogel, Rivka, 91–92

fuite en avant, 117

Gazeta Pomorska (newspaper), 88

Gazeta Wyborcza (newspaper), 137

Geniek, Kozłowski, 18

German occupation (1941): communist sympathizers denounced during, 55–56; Finkelsztajn testimony on, 57–69; Jewish pogroms during, 56; Kupiechki, Wiśniewski brothers murdered during,

56; Polish friendly response to, 152–154, 245n.3; prohibitions concerning Jews during, 132–133. *See also* collaboration; World War II

German-Soviet Boundary and Friendship Treaty (1939), 42

German-Soviet Treaty of Non-Aggression (1939), 10, 41–42

Germany: *Armes Deutschland* response by, 144–145; Boundary and Friendship Treaty with USSR, 42; controversy over German army's role in Holocaust in, 145; Jedwabne occupation by, 10, 42; Non-Aggression Treaty with USSR, 10, 41–42; sense of victimization by, 243n.2. *See also* Gestapo; Nazis

Gerwad, Mieczysław, 73

Gestapo: additional testimonies on, 227n.7; Bardoń testimony on role by, 84–85; Śliwecki testimony on role by, 226n.6; Sokołwska testimony on role by, 74–76, 77–78. *See also* Nazis

Ghetto Archive (*Oneg Shabbat*), 213n.4

Głowiński, Michał, 134, 239n.2

Gościcki, Wincenty, 93, 96, 102

Grądowski, Eliasz, 105
Grot-Rowecki, General (AK forces), 152
Grynberg, Henryk, 129
Grzymkowski, Stanisław, 67

Hamburg Institute for Social Research, 145
Heydrich, Reinhardt, 132
Historical Bureau of the Anders Army: Borawski testimony kept by, 48–51; Soviet occupation questionnaires of, 43
historiography: challenging standard Jedwabne massacre, 138–142; challenging standard World War II, 7–8; Holocaust, 11–12; of Polish martyrology, 143–151; regarding *szmalcownicy* collaborators, 8, 139
Hitler, Adolf, 3, 4, 6, 10, 41, 78, 152
Hochheiser, Izzy, 158, 159
Hochheiser, Sally, 158, 159
Hochheiser, Sammy, 158
Holocaust: *Armes Deutschland* ("Poor Germany") response to, 144–145; controversy over German army's role in, 145; functionalist-intentionalist spectrum of, 11–12; as heterogeneous phenomenon, 124–125; inability to attain closure on, 12–13; Jewish testimonies recording the, 24–26, 141–142; Polish demographic catastrophe from, 6–7. *See also* Jewish pogroms; The Shoah phenomenon

Ibram, Judes, 96
Institute of National Memory, 172

Janowaki, Irena, 112
Janowska, Aleksander, 112
Jedwabne: anti-Soviet underground in, 47–53; fires historically plaguing, 33–34; history of Jewish population in, 34–35, 218nn.2 and 4; impact of Soviet occupation on, 54–55; incidents of anti-semitism in, 38–39; Jewish families seeking refuge in, 70–71; location of, 33; occupations of Jewish population in, 35–36; prewar Polish-Jewish relations in, 37–38, 212n.3, 218n.2; recorded reception of Soviets in, 45–47; shifting Soviet/Nazi occupation of, 10, 42–53; Soviet administration officials in, 44; stigma attached to aiding the Jews in, 130–131; wartime population of, 15. *See also* Jadwabne massacre (July 1941)

Jedwabne Jewry memorial book, 34, 140
Jedwabne Jews (*Jedwabne Krichers*), 36
Jedwabne massacre (July 1941): advance knowledge/warnings of, 72–73, 90, 226n.2; arrests (1949) following, 112–113, 208n.1; burial of victims of, 102–103; challenging standard historiography of, 138–142; common knowledge regarding, 226n.6; destruction of anti-Soviet underground and, 47–53; events just prior to, 54–55; eyewitness accounts on cruelty of, 88–89, 91–103; few survivors of, 103–104; German photographic record of, 78, 79, 80, 211n.2; Gestapo role in, 74–76, 77–78, 226n.6, 227n.7; Jewish property plundered during, 105–110; Jews burned alive in Śleszyński's barn, 19–20, 89, 98, 99–101, 229n.9; "leftover" Jewish property motive behind, 105–107, 110, 234n.4; locating documentation on, 23–32; mayor/town council complicity in, 73–76; official investigation of, 29–30; participants in, 86–88; Polish awareness of, 22, 28–29; Polish-Jewish relations context of, 7; *Raport likwidacyjny* (liquidation report) on, 14–15; reopening investigation (2000) of, 172–173; stigma attached to aiding Jews during, 130–131; two stone monuments commemorating, 169–170; Wasersztajn's testimony describing, 15–22, 24, 97, 101, 140. See also Jewish pogroms

Jedwabne massacre documentation: Bardoń's confessional text, 113–114; eyewitness accounts as, 88–89, 91–103; from court trials, 26–32, 214n.5; Jerzy Laudański's petition, 118–120; Jewish testimonies as, 24–25; JHI (Jewish Historical Institute) collection of, 15, 21, 57, 97, 141, 158, 210n.6; Niełatwicki testimony on, 70, 71, 72, 73, 93–94, 211n.2, 225n.1, 232n.13; petitions from wives of arrested men, 112–113; search for, 23–24, 209n.5; on stigma attached to aiding Jews, 130–131; two stone monuments as, 169–170; Wasersztajn's testimony as, 15–22, 24, 97, 101, 140, 141; Zygmunt Laudański's petition, 114–116

Jedwabne massacre participants: arrests (1949) of, 111, 208n.1; confessions by, 216n.6; described, 86–88; description of speech by, 118; Laudański petition from, 114–116; as "ordinary men," 120–121; petitions from wives (1949) of, 112–113; Soviet and German collaboration by, 16–20, 115–118, 163; trial verdicts on, 27, 214n.5

Jedwabne massacre trial: community amnesia during, 28; defendant confessions/appeals during, 29, 79–85, 111, 216n.6, 217n.10; demeanor of witness/defendants during, 81–82; deposition on mayor/town council complicity, 73–76; documentation from, 26–32, 214n.5; haste and verdicts in, 27, 214n.5. See also Jedwabne massacre documentation

Jermałowski, 18

Jewish collective memory: on free will/responsibility for violence, 133–135; on violence against Jews, 122–123, 235n.1

Jewish pogroms: conducted by local free will, 132–134; illustration of, 231n.1; Kielce (1946), 148, 149, 236nn.2

and 3; ritual murder belief as trigger for, 123–124, 150, 236n.1; in surrounding villages, 70–71; testimony on Radziłow (July 1941), 57–69; in Wąsosz, 69, 70. See also antisemitism; Holocaust; Jedwabne massacre (July 1941)

Jewish population: alleged Soviet collaboration by, 10–11, 46–47, 155, 246n.11; collective memory on violence against, 122–123, 133–135; German prohibiting assistance to, 133; history of Jedwabne, 34–35, 218nn.2 and 4; Holocaust catastrophe suffered by, 6–7; Holocaust catastrophe suffered by Polish, 6–7; occupations of Jedwabne, 35–36; prewar boundaries of existence by, 39–40; pre–World War II, 8; recorded reception of Soviets by, 45–47; Shoah episodes testimonies by, 24–25, 57–69; sources of violence against, 123–125; during Soviet occupation, 43–53; stigma attaching to those aiding, 129–131, 238n.3; vulnerable to antisemitism by, 38–39; World War II historiography of, 8. See also Polish-Jewish relations

Jewish property, 105–107, 110, 234n.4

Jewish testimonies: by Aharon Appelfeld, 126–128; by Chajcia Wasersztajn, 15–22, 24, 97, 101, 130, 140, 141; by Cracow pogrom victim, 149–150; JHI collection of Holocaust, 141; by Karolcia Sapetowa, 158–161; by Menachem Finkelsztajn, 57–69, 141, 155, 224n.5, 225n.6; by Niełąwicki, 70, 71, 72, 73, 93–94, 211n.2, 225n.1, 232n.13; as obligation to record evidence, 24–25; principle affirmative approach to, 139–142; recording the Holocaust, 24–26, 141–142; on Righteous Gentiles, 238n.3; by Rivka Fogel, 91–92; survivor perspective of, 141–142; by Szmul Wasersztajn, 15–22, 24, 97, 101, 140. *See also* documentation

JHI (Jewish Historical Institute), 15, 21, 57, 97, 141, 158, 210n.6

Kac, Jakub, 16
Kaczyński, Andrzej, 171, 172
Kalinowska, Bronisława, 97
Kalinowski, Eugeniusz, 77, 81, 95, 100
Kamiński, Łukasz, 147
Karolak, Marian, 18, 72, 74, 77, 85, 91, 94, 107, 109, 110

Karwowska, Aleksandra, 102
Karwowski, Kazimierz, 106
Kersten, Krystyna, 157, 244n.3
Khmielnicki's peasant wars, 123
Khurban (foreshadowing of Shoah), 123
Kielce pogrom (1946), 148, 149, 236nn.2 and 3
Klukowski, Zygmunt, 160
Kobrzyniecki, Józef, 101–102, 106, 233n.25
Kobrzyniecki brothers, 101–102, 106
Kolno Jews (*Kolner Pekelach-Pekewach*), 36
Komsomol (Organization of Communist Youth), 44
Korboński, Stefan, 147
Kosak, 63
Kosmaczewski, Józef Anton, 63
Kosmaczewski, Leon, 63
Kovaly, Heda, 6
Kozłowski, Gienek, 105
Kozłowski, Mr., 88
Krawiecki, Eliasz, 16
Krystowczyk, Henryk, 75, 108
Krystowczyk, Zygmunt, 108
Kubrzańska, Chaja, 17
Kubrzański, Janek, 131
Kupiecki, Czesław, 55, 56, 224n.4
Kuropatwa, Michał, 99

Laciecz, Czesław, 18
Laudański, Czesław, 99
Laudański, Jerzy, 18, 74, 76, 95, 97, 109, 117, 118–120
Laudański, Zygmunt, 74, 114–116, 165
Laudański brothers, 106
Laudański family, 109
Laudański (Jerzy) petition (1949), 118–120
Laudański (Zygmunt) petition (1949), 114–116
"leftover" Jewish property, 105–107, 110, 234n.4
Lenin, Vladimir Ilich, 167
Lewin, Joseph, 92, 95, 96
Lewiniuk, 89
Lewinowicz, 52
Lipiński, Czesław, 76, 230n.12
Łódź Thread Factory, 148
Łomża Jews (*Lomzer Baaloonim*), 36
Łomża Security Office investigation, 29–30
Łomża Yeshiva, 37
Łoziński, Paweł, 128
Łuba, Władysław, 96

Majecki, Henryk, 44
Malinowski, 70
Malyshev, Aleksandr Nikiforovich, 44
material expropriation motive, 105–107, 110, 234n.4
Matujewicz, Grzegorz, 29
Mazurek, Jan, 64
Miciura, Władysław, 77, 86, 87
Mierzejewski, Czesław, 96
Mierzwa, Stanisław, 147
Mikołajczyk, Stanisław, 147
Misiuriew (NKVD colonel), 52, 115, 156
Moishe, Reb Nachum, 36
Molotov, Vyacheslav, 41
Mordaszewicz, Feliks, 63
MTS (Mechinical Tractor Station), 114
"My Biography for 1940–1941" (Borawski), 48–51

Nadolny (Nadolnik), Gitele, 96
national heritage/identity. *See* Polish collective identity
Nazis: collaboration relationship with, 4–5; Jedwabne massacre ordered by, 17–18; postwar retribution against, 5–6. *See also* Gestapo
Neumark, Janek, 100
Niebrzydowski, Antoni, 99–100
Niebrzydowski, Jerzy, 100
Nieławicki, Wiktor, 70, 71, 72, 73, 93–94, 211n.2, 225n.1, 232n.13
NKVD (Soviet secret police), 47, 50, 52, 115, 116, 170
NSZ (National Armed Forces). *See* Polish underground

Olszewicz, Mietek, 72, 94
Oneg Shabbat initiative (Ringelblum), 25, 213n.4
Ordinary Men (Browning), 120
Ordnungspolizei Batallion no. 101, 120

Pecynowicz, Dvojra, 71, 72
Piekarz, Hershel, 151
The Place of Birth (film documentary), 128–129
Poland: Communist rule (1945–1948)/Stalinism of, 164–167; examining collective identity of, 135–137; invaded by USSR (1939), 42; moral disintegration of, 157–163; political sympathies of Catholic clergy in, 219n.9; post–World War II antsemitism, 150–151; post–World War II workers' strikes in, 147–149; World War II demographic catastrophe suffered by, 6–7. *See also* German occupation (1941); Polish population; Soviet occupation (1939–1941)
Polish Association for Insurrection (Polski Zwizek Powstańczy), 119
Polish collective identity: common historical experiences and, 135; impact of mass murder on, 136–137; selectivity in creating authentic, 135–136; wartime martyrology as part of, 143–151
Polish Communism: antisemitic role in, 167, 247n.3; nature of people supporting, 164–166
Polish Communist Party, 164–167
Polish Countryside, 1939–1948 (Kersten and Szarota), 157–158
Polish-Jewish relations: antisemitism as part of, 38–39; assigning responsibility in, 133–135; autonomous dynamics in, 9–10; boundaries of prewar, 39–40; challenging historiography of, 138–142; Finkelsztajn testimony relating, 58–69; inherent danger for Jews in, 133–134; Jedwabne massacre in context of, 7; Polish moral disintegration and, 157–163; post–World War II, 146–151; recollections of prewar Jedwabne, 37–38, 212n.3, 218n.2; reconciling Polish martyrology with, 143–151; during Soviet occupation, 43–53
Polish Jewry. *See* Jewish population
Polish population: friendly reception to German army by,

Polish population (cont.)
152–154, 245n.3; impact of
totalitarianism on, 157–161;
Jewish pogroms conducted
by, 132–134; moral disintegration of, 157–163; responsible participation in atrocities by, 242n.1; Soviet
deportation of, 217n.9,
220n.2. See also Jedwabne
massacre participants;
Poland
Polish underground: activities
near Jedwabne by, 47, 83,
228n.7, 229n.8; Jedwabne
massacre and destruction of,
47–53; Jerzy Laudański's
membership in, 119; on Polish reception to Germany
army, 152–154; Soviet collaborators within, 155–156
Polish workers' strikes: following Kielce pogrom, 148–
149; Kamiński's research
on, 147–149
Polkowska, Anna, 106
Popiołek, Halina, 88
PPR (Polish Workers' Party),
108, 116, 117
PPS (Polish Socialist Party),
147
Pravde, Mrs., 92
PSL (Polish Peasant Party),
147
Pyontkowski, Aryeh, 35–36
Pyontkowski, Nachum
Moishe, 35–36

"A Quarter-Hour Passed in a
Pastry Shop" (Głowiński
memoir), 134

Radziłów Jews (Radzilower
Kozes), 36
Radziłów pogrom (July 1941),
57–69, 97, 140
Radziłów Polish population,
155
raion party committee, 44
Ramotowski, Bolesław: on
German photographing of
massacre, 79; on number of
massacre participants, 86–
87; phrasing of accusation
against, 29–30; Sokołowska
testimony against, 80; trial
of, 15, 27, 154
Ramotowski, Stanisław, 69–70
Ramotowski trial. See Jed-
wabne massacre trial
Ramutowski, Bolek, 18
Raport likwidacyjny (liquidation
report), 14–15
Reznel[?], Moses, 67
Ribbentrop, Joachim von, 41
Ribbentrop-Molotov Pact
(1939), 10, 41–42
Righteous Amongst Nations,
129, 238n.3
Ringelblum, Emanuel, 25
Ringelblum Archive (Oneg
Shabbat group), 25, 213n.4
ritual murder belief, 123–124,
150, 236n.1
Rogalski, Bolek, 18

Rothchild, Jona, 39
Rothchild, Tsiporah, 35
Russo-German War (1941),
54, 132
Rydachenko, Mark Timofee-
vich, 44
Rzeczpospolita newspaper, 171

Sapetowa, Karolcia, 158–161
Secret Additional Protocol
(Ribbentrop-Molotov Pact),
42
The Shoah phenomenon: con-
text of, 207n.12; *Khurban*
(foreshadowing) of, 123; as
rooted in modernity, 124–
125; testimonies on, 24–25.
See also Holocaust; Jewish
pogroms
Sielawa, Stanisław, 106, 107,
219n.5
Sielawa, Staszek, 100, 107,
219n.5
Sienkiewicz, Henryk, 122
Śleszyńska, Rozalia, 106, 171
Śleszyński, Bronisław, 22, 79
Śleszyński, Edward, 79, 101
Śleszyński's barn: Jews buried
alive in, 19–20, 89, 98, 99–
101, 229n.9; rebuilt by Ger-
mans, 107–109
Śliwecki, Eugeniusz, 226n.6
Sobieski, Jan, 136
Sobuta, Józef, 27, 55–56, 72,
91, 98, 106, 107, 215n.5,
225n.1, 234n.4
Sobuta, Stanisława, 106

Sokołowska, Julia, 79–82, 83,
84, 106
Soviet-Jewish relations: alleged collaboration in, 46–
47, 155, 246n.11; current
stereotype of, 10–11
Soviet occupation (1939–
1941): alleged Jewish collaboration during, 10–11, 46–
47, 155, 246n.11; Bardoń's
official positions under,
113–114; deportation of
Poles during, 217n.9,
220n.2; five most important
officials of, 44; impact on
Jedwabne by, 54–55; investi-
gative/judiciary authorities
during, 28; of Jedwabne,
42–53; Jedwabne anti-Soviet
underground during, 47–53;
Laudański's (Zygmunt) petition on collaboration during, 114–117; linkage be-
tween Jedwabne massacre
and, 10; Polish response to
ending of, 152–154; Polish-
Soviet collaboration during,
155–157; recorded Jed-
wabne reception of, 45–47.
See also USSR; World War
II
Stalin, Joseph, 3, 4, 6, 10, 41,
115
Stefany, Fredek, 106
Strzembosz, Tomasz, 21, 47
Sukachov, Danil Kireyevich,
44

Szarota, Tomasz, 157, 244n.3
Szczebrzeszyn Jews, 161–162
Szelawa, Franciszek, 18
Szelawa, Stanisław, 18, 97
Szlepen [?], Wolf, 62, 68
Szleziński, Bronisław, 18
szmalcownicy, 8, 139, 207n.10
Szumowski, Father Marian, 40

Tarnacki, Feliks, 77
Tarnoczek, Jerzyk, 18
testimonies. *See* Jewish testimonies
totalitarianism: crippling impact of, 4; implemented by Hitler and Stalin, 3; logic of collaboration incentives in, 117–118; pattern of occupation imposed by, 4–5; type of individual supporting, 165–166, 246n.1; World War II exposure of Poland to, 157–161
Treaty of Non-Aggression Pact of 1939 (Germany-USSR), 10, 41–42
trial. *See* Jedwabne massacre trial
Trilogy (Sienkiewicz), 123
Trzaska, 18

UB (*Urząd Bezpieczeństwa*), 28
Urbanowski, 93
USSR: Boundary and Friendship Treaty with Germany, 42; German *Blitzkrieg* (1941) against, 152–153; invasion of Poland (1939) by, 42; Non-Aggression Treaty with Germany, 10, 41–42; Polish occupation by, 10, 42. *See also* Soviet occupation (1939–1941)
Ustilovski, Dymitri Borisovich, 44

Vernichtungskrieg, Verbrechen der Wehrmacht 1941 bis 1944 controversy, 145
Voegelin, Eric, 156

Warsaw Uprising (1944), 137
Wasersztajn, Chajcia, 16, 130, 140, 141
Wasersztajn, Szmul, 15, 16, 24, 97
Wasersztajn deposition: on the Jedwabne massacre, 15–20, 24, 97, 140, 141; meaning of, 21–22; testimony confirming truth of, 101
Weszezewski[?], Ludwik, 63, 72, 77, 98
Where Is My Older Brother Cain? (documentary film), 22, 171, 211n.7, 230n.17
"Wiarus" ("Old Veteran"), 83
Wiśniewski, 49, 50, 56, 92, 95
Wiśniewski (brother), 56
Wizna pogrom, 69, 70
Workers' Strikes in Poland in the Years 1945–1948 (Kamiński), 147, 148–149

World War II: political/social legacy of, 6–7; Ribbentrop-Molotov Pact (1939) as beginning of, 10, 41–42. *See also* collaboration; German occupation (1941); Soviet occupation (1939–1941)

World War II historiography: *Armes Deutschland* ("Poor Germany") response and, 144–145; challenging Jedwabne massacre, 138–142; challenging the standard, 7–8; Holocaust, 11–12; regarding *szmalcownicy* collaborators, 8

Wyka, Kazimierz, 157

Wyrzykowski, Aleksander, 130–131

Wyrzykowski, Antonia, 130–131

Wyrzykowski family, 104, 129–131, 151

Yad Vashem authority, 129

Zdrojewicz, Hersh, 95, 96

ZSCh (peasant cooperative), 108

Żuławski, Zygmunt, 147

Żyluk, Janina, 112–113

Żyluk, Józef, 76

Also by
JAN T. GROSS

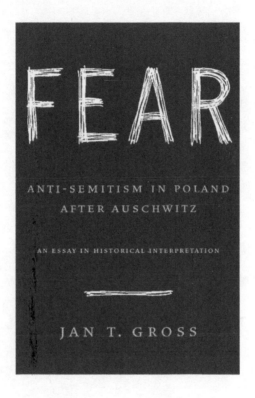

⫿P PRINCETON UNIVERSITY PRESS

Available wherever books are sold.
For more information visit us at www.press.princeton.edu